NOTE-TAKING

FOR

PUBLIC SERVICE

INTERPRETERS

Kirsty Heimerl-Moggan & Vanessa Ifeoma John

To order further copies of this book or any of our other publications please contact us direct at:

Interp-Right Training Consultancy Ltd.
9 Capesthorne Road
Timperley
Altrincham
Cheshire
WA15 7EA

T: +44 (0) 161 980 0434
F: +44 (0) 161 980 7834

www.interp-right.com
interpright@btinternet.com

Published by Interp-Right Training Consultancy Ltd.

TABLE OF CONTENTS

ACKNOWLEDGEMENTS

Special thanks must be given to my parents – the best I could ever wish for. By helping me pursue the career I had always dreamed of, they have made all of this possible. Special thoughts go to my grandmother who, for as long as I can remember, has been my constant inspiration.
But most of all I have to thank my wonderful husband; without his patience, guidance and support this book would never have happened.
Mention must also be made of Mrs. Gross-Dinter and Mr. Dinter, the two people who started my 'note-taking career' at the Sprachen- und Dolmetscher-Institut in Munich. I am sure they will recognise how strong their influence has been.
Thanks also go to the late Andrew Riddell from the University of Salford, who further refined my note-taking skills.
Finally I would like to turn to those interpreting students I have taught over the years. Their suggestions have inspired many of my symbols, and hopefully these will go on to inspire many more students in the years to come.

Kirsty Heimerl-Moggan

To my inspiration and guiding light - my mother. It was she who realised my interest and potential in interpreting long before I did. It was she who always encouraged me to believe in myself the way she did and to work hard to achieve what often seemed too far out of reach. I thank her for the sacrifices she made for me and for showing me how to make my own. Looking back, I wonder how we managed.
A big thank you also to Guadalupe Canales and Maria Sanchez for encouraging me to tackle Spanish interpreting.

Vanessa Ifeoma John

ABOUT THE AUTHORS

Kirsty Heimerl-Moggan

Kirsty Heimerl-Moggan works as a Conference Interpreter and Public Service Interpreter and is based both in Munich, Germany, and in the North West of England. She is a full member of the National Register of Public Service Interpreters and holds the German equivalent of the BA in Legal Interpreting. In 1996 Kirsty gained her Masters Degree in Conference Interpreting at the University of Salford, with her dissertation investigating interpreter stresses in both Public Service and Conference Interpreting.

Kirsty has worked as a part-time lecturer in Conference Interpreting at MA and BA level (both into and out of German) at Salford University. She is now a guest lecturer in interpreting at various universities. As a qualified Adult and Further Education teacher, she has been teaching the English Law, Local Government and Health options of the Diploma in Public Service Interpreting since 1998. Kirsty also trains interpreters for the Immigration Nationality Directorate, the Institute of Translators and Interpreters (ITI) and various major commercial clients. She has also served as a member of the interview panel for the Metropolitan Police Service Interpreter List.

She has worked as a board member of the Interpreting Division of the Institute of Linguists and is a full member of the Chartered Institute of Linguists (IoL), the Institute of Translators and Interpreters (ITI), the Association of Police & Court Interpreters (APCI) and the North West Translator's Network (NWTN).

Kirsty's previous publications include two client-information booklets on commissioning conference interpreting and business interpreting; a series of 10 Top Tips on Working with Interpreters (e.g. Conference Interpreters, Business Interpreters, and Interpreters working with Criminal Justice Officers, Legal Professionals, Local Government Officers, Prison Officers, Probation Officers, Immigration Officers and Emergency Service Officers) and an additional 10 Top Tips for Prison Interpreters themselves.

Vanessa Ifeoma John

Vanessa Ifeoma John works as a Conference and Public Service Interpreter, Translator and Interpreting Trainer specialising in Note-taking for both Conference and Public Service Interpreting. She is based both in Berlin, Germany, and in the North West of England.
She holds a BA in Modern Languages, Translating and Interpreting Studies for German, Spanish and English from Salford University. In 2007 she gained her MA in Translation and Interpreting for German, Spanish and English at the same University with her dissertation investigating the difficulties in transferring ethnically placed English into German. In the same year she also obtained her Diploma in Public Service Interpreting (Law Option).

Vanessa works as a part-time lecturer in Conference Interpreting at MA and BA level at the University of Salford and trains interpreters and translators for various organisations such as Interp-Right Training Consultancy Ltd. She is a DPSI Law Option Trainer and works as a German / English Teacher and Tutor.

Vanessa's roles have involved her both interpreting and acting as an expert observing interpreter on difficult cases.

FOREWORD

As described by Mark Shuttleworth and Moira Cowie in their *Dictionary of Translation Studies*, 'interpreters need to be expert oral communicators, and are required to create a finished product in "real time" without the possibility of going back and making revisions' (1997:84). This is the case in Public Service Interpreting, in environments such as a hospital, a police station, a court room or a prison establishment. Here, the interpreter deals with facts and situations where details are crucial and need to be transferred across to another language with clarity and precision.

Shuttleworth and Cowie also refer to interpreters 'as "performers" who are constantly making split-second decisions and taking communicative risks' (1997:84). These risks however need to be minimised. And to do so the interpreter must be extremely well prepared and use all of his/her skills – linguistic and memorative – as well as any tools that will assist in his/her performance. One such tool is note-taking to assist with details during interpreting. The ability to note-take effectively is therefore vital if this aid-memoir is to prove useful in assisting the interpreter.

Effective note-taking is a skill in its own right, one which requires the development of a specific set of symbols and techniques and a considerable amount of practice. Mastering this skill is paramount to the interpreter and therefore the publication of this innovative manual is a welcome development for the interpreting profession.

Cristina Sousa

Dr. Cristina Sousa
RLN NW Ltd.

INTRODUCTION

The stimulus for the writing of this book came not from ourselves, the authors, but from our respective students. So many of our public service interpreting students, when introduced to note-taking for the first time, would ask if there were an accessible handbook available which would give them practical suggestions for using note-taking during their public service interpreting assignments.

We therefore decided to incorporate our respective teaching materials and our first-hand experience of the practical problems encountered by our students into the book which you now have in your hands.

We have tried to make this a practical handbook rather than an academic textbook, as there are already many good academic publications on note-taking on the market.

One of our foremost considerations in its production has been to attempt to use the tried-and-tested approaches to note-taking found in conference interpreting (where note-taking is much more established) and to adapt them to public service interpreting (where note-taking is still somewhat in its infancy).

We are firmly convinced that note-taking is, like a lot of things in life, a skill whereby the more effort you put in to it, the more you will get out of it. We are also convinced that it is worth all the effort you can afford to give it. Time spent in perfecting your own set of unique symbols will pay great dividends in helping you with your interpreting. At first you may not find it easy, but stick with it and it will become progressively easier. To this day we still get a great thrill every time one of our students exclaims, "It really works, I never thought I'd say it but it really works." We sincerely hope that you will stick at and eventually reap all the benefits which it has to offer.

CHAPTER 1

NOTE-TAKING – WHAT IS IT AND WHY DO IT?

What Is Note-Taking?

- Note-taking is a method used by interpreters to jot down information which they are hearing in order to subsequently transfer it into another language.

Why Do Note-Taking?

- As an interpreter you have to memorise the information you hear in order to be able to reproduce that same information in the target language.

- The already complex process of interpreting can often be made even more difficult by various factors such as:

    - Speakers continuing to speak for long periods of time (this could be for reasons such as emotional involvement or a lack of understanding of the interpreting process).

    - The speakers' words, for various reasons, not always making sense to the interpreter.

    - When a list of items is being recounted.

    - When the speaker is upset.

    - When the speaker repeats the same basic information several times but uses slightly different sentence constructions each time they do so.

- Note-taking is a memory aid which makes retrieval of information for interpretation purposes easier.

- It also guarantees correct relaying of the information heard e.g. correct order, completeness and clarity.

Why Do Note-Taking In Public Service Interpreting?

- Not all Public Service Interpreters use note-taking as a memory aid but those who do
    - Find it extremely useful.
    - Are more efficient.
    - Ensure that they can interpret everything correctly.

- It is as important for Public Service Interpreters to be able to convey the information accurately as it is for any other interpreter – sometimes even more so e.g. when a patient's life depends on the correct interpretation of the doctor's instruction on how to take medication, or when a person's freedom is at stake as in police interviews or court proceedings.

- Most Public Service Interpreters do note-taking mixed with other memory-aiding techniques and each individual will have a very different approach to noting down information.

- It is found particularly useful by interpreters as they have to concentrate slightly less on remembering the exact order of the information (as they have it noted down to refer back to it when rendering the information) and they can devote more time to ensuring that they convey the exact tone, register, intonation etc. of the speaker – which is an essential part of 100% communication.

- It is, however, clear that those interpreters using their pads and note-taking are much more likely to convey the correct information in the correct order.

CHAPTER 2

MEMORY SKILLS AND NOTE-TAKING

Memory Skills

Before we start looking at how note-taking is done, it is important to remember that note-taking can only work together with memory / retention skills.

There are various exercises you can use, not only to enhance your short-term memory in general, but also to improve your approach to remembering those parts of the information which you do not note down on your interpreting pad. Figures and plain facts are a lot more difficult to remember than a sequence of connected events. These exercises are meant to help you retain information that is more abstract.

General Exercises

- During the day try and remember the number plate, make and colour of five cars you have seen without writing any of it down or confusing which plate belonged to which car.

- Make a glossary of all countries and their capitals with their respective abbreviations (i.e. international number plate code for the countries and airport code for the capitals) and international dialling codes. Now every time you mention or hear either of them, recall the information connected to it. Hence, if your colleague says they went on holiday to France, you could recall: FR, CDG, +0033.

- Change your habits! If, for example, you always use a certain route to work and back, use a different one every so often. Change challenges your brain.

- Listen to the news on the radio in the morning and recall the events a few times during the day. This will not only improve your memory but also your general knowledge of current affairs.

- Each night when you lie down and have just turned off the lights, take 5 minutes to go through your day again. Try and visualise yourself experiencing the entire day focusing on details.

Specific Exercises

- Work with two of your colleagues. Assign one person to recount an incident. You should count aloud from 1 to 100 in English. The third person checks on you to ensure you do not miscount. At the same time you should also be listening to the story, as you will have to re-tell the story afterwards. This will help you to split your attention between counting on the one hand and listening and memorising on the other.
  This exercise can be extended in the following way:
  - Try to count backwards from 100 to 1
  - The exercise can be done bilingually, i.e. listening and counting in one language and re-telling in another

- When listening to a taped speech, count the information you hear, i.e. break the string of information down into individual items – these would be exactly those items you would note down in symbols on your note pad – and count them either in your mind or on your fingers. After the speaker has finished, list the individual items as numbers on a sheet of paper leaving sufficient space between each item. Now try and reconstruct the speech event in your mind firstly by connecting the items from 1 - 10. and then by filling in the gaps on your sheet of paper. Then double check with the tape.

- When listening to someone speaking, visualise what you hear as it is simpler to remember information which you 'see' rather than something which you hear. For example, if the speaker says, "I went to the shop," imagine that action, maybe even yourself taking your normal route to your local shop, if this helps you to visualise it better. This way, all you will have to note down on your pad is your symbol for *shop*. Then, when you render what you heard based on the symbol, you will *see* the person actually walking to the shop simply by looking at the shop symbol because you have triggered a visual memory of what you heard.

CHAPTER 3

NOTE-TAKING – HOW IS IT DONE?

How Is Note-Taking Done?

- Note-taking is the process of noting down the information you hear in the quickest way possible.
- In order to achieve this goal it would be virtually impossible to write everything down in full.
- It is essential therefore to locate those words in each sentence which have *meaning* i.e. those words that are important to the *message*. These are sometimes referred to as *meaning* words.

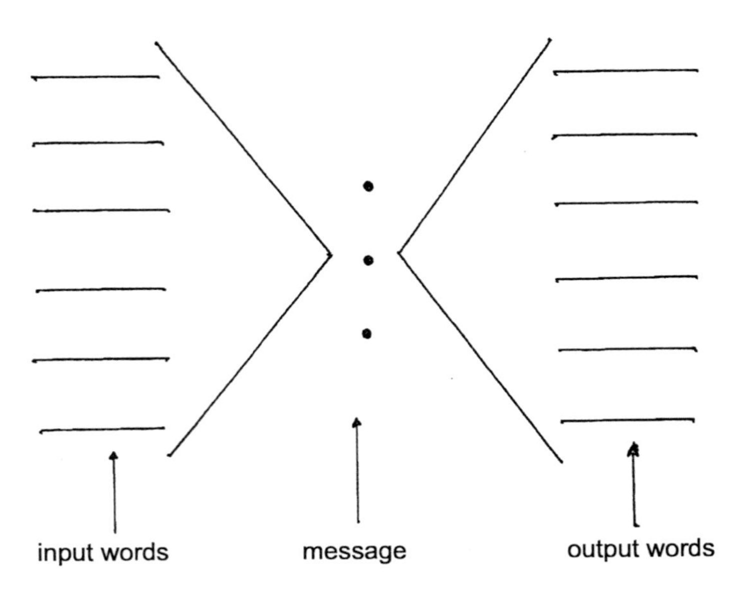

- However, writing down even just the important words would still take too long.

- So instead of writing down full words an interpreter doing note-taking will use
    - Abbreviations
    - Acronyms

    but mainly
    - Symbols

- The *perfect* approach to note-taking would be to use only symbols.

- From the outset it is essential that interpreters are taught the skills and given the tools necessary to start developing their own personal set of note-taking symbols.

- Once an interpreter has been equipped with the essential basic skills and ideas of note-taking they then have to start working on their own individual set of symbols.

- Interpreters can work together on developing their own symbols but they need to be aware that another interpreter's symbols may not work for them and vice versa.

- Developing symbols is a first step in the note-taking process. Once a set of symbols has been developed the interpreter must then try to use these symbols to see if they *work*. A symbol *works* if:

    - It can be remembered by the interpreter in the heat of the moment i.e. when the symbols are being jotted down during the interpreting assignment.

    - It is always used for the expression for which it has been developed.

    - It becomes a long-term, established symbol in the interpreter's set of notes.

- Regular practice and updating are a vital part of becoming a successful note-taker and are useful

    - for the purpose of reinforcing symbols that have already been developed, but which may have been forgotten.

    - when working on topics in preparation for types of assignment which are new to the interpreter.

    - so as not to fall back into *bad* behaviours e.g. writing words out in full.

- Note-taking practice should become an integral part of the interpreter's Continuous Professional Development (CPD).

How Does Note-Taking Not Work?

- Note-taking does not replace the following processes of interpreting:
    - Listening
    - Understanding
    - Memorising

- Note-taking is simply an aide-mémoire, in other words a crutch for your brain.

- Your notes are a product of the moment i.e. they should merely trigger your memory of something that you have just heard.

- If an interpreter were to look at their notes a week or even just a few days after the assignment they may not be able to read them, as without the benefit of the words being fresh in their mind, their notes may not make much sense.

- Developing note-taking symbols should take place before and after the assignment or at other times, but not during the interpreting assignment. It takes time to think of symbols and it would impact negatively on the interpreter's performance if they attempted to do it during the assignment. The time taken would seriously detract from the listening and understanding process.

- It cannot be denied that interpreters do sometimes think of a symbol during an assignment on the spur of the moment, which they then start using all the time, but this is not the norm.

Remember: **Note-taking is aimed solely at helping your memory – if you have not listened properly and have not memorised most of what has been said, then no amount of symbols will help you interpret!**

CHAPTER 4

NOTE-TAKING – YOUR PRACTICE STARTS HERE

Starting Note-Taking

- Firstly it is important to ensure that the interpreter has the correct tools:

Tools For Note-Taking

- Pens – it is essential to have several pens (they always run out at the most inconvenient times).

- Choose your writing tool by ensuring you use the one with which you feel most comfortable and with which you can write the fastest – for some people pencils are much faster than pens.

- The interpreter's pad
    - The pad that is used by most interpreters is a reporter's note-book (roughly A5 size). The great advantage of the A5 pad is that if you write on only one side of the paper the pages can be turned over relatively quietly during an assignment and when the pad is full it can then simply be turned over and you can carry on writing on the reverse of the pages.

    - Some interpreters use A5 or A4 clipboards with paper – the danger here is that the pages may come loose.

    - A4 pads are also used by interpreters but unlike A5 pads the pages have a tendency to become worn when being carried from assignment to assignment and transferred from bag to bag. The other disadvantage is that A4 pages tend to make a noise when being turned over and this can be distracting during an assignment.

- A note-taking folder – many interpreters have a small ringbinder or note-book in which they collect the symbols which they have developed.

- Ringbinders can be more useful as items can be added into any section.
- Filing systems are either alphabetical or according to topic areas, but most of the time a mix of both filing systems is used.

The Best Way To Use Your Pad

Splitting the page vertically

- Splitting up the page into a small section on the left side and a large section on the right side is a useful idea.

- This approach makes it possible to clearly differentiate between the types of information which are being noted down.

- This, of course, requires preparation of your interpreting pad in advance by drawing in the separating line.

- When it is not possible to prepare your pad in advance adhere to a fictitious line, i.e. take down the information in the same way you would as if you had already drawn in the line.

Splitting the page vertically

Section 1	**Section 2**
Small section	Large section
Small section	Large section
Small section	Large section
Small section	Large section
Small section	Large section

Splitting the page horizontally

Section 1	**Section 2**
Part 1	Part 1
Part 2	Part 2
Part 3	Part 3
Part 4	Part 4
Part 5	Part 5

What To Write In The Small Section On Your Pages

- For link words i.e. words that connect the individual ideas or sentences,
  e.g.

Section 1	Section 2
and, because, as while, although, due to, in order to etc.	

- Identifying the person concerned e.g. the speaker or someone the speaker may be referring to,
  e.g.

Section 1	Section 2
I, he, she, defendant, judge, police officer etc.	

- If the sentence in section 2 is a question, it should be marked in section 1 by using a question mark. In this way the interpreter knows immediately that the information in section 2 has to be rendered in the form of a question, i.e. the intonation and the sentence structure have to be changed. Also used for exclamations etc.

Section 1	Section 2
? or !	

- Stating opinion or similar (abbreviations for such terms will be discussed at a later stage)

Section 1	Section 2
I am pleased to be here, It is sad to see, I was frightened to see, etc.	

- Time indicators can be noted in section 1

Section 1	Section 2
1996, last year, in two days, today etc.	

- Heading of new chapters/categories, which should be made clear.

Section 1	Section 2
What happened at the crime scene, while he was in the ambulance etc.	

A More Detailed Look At The Left Hand Side Of The Page

Times and Dates

Note down any time indicator such as a certain date, time of day, period of time, etc. to draw your own attention to these indicators. Again, these can be vital to what a person is saying, although they might not necessarily form part of the main idea. It is absolutely vital to decide on and stick to a certain format of noting down dates and times of day so as not to confuse yourself at the time of interpretation (e.g. using the 24hr or am/pm time format or using dd/mm/yy or mm/dd/yy or using letter abbreviations for the months, etc.).

Salutations And Names Of People Greeted

Every speech event has a beginning and usually this beginning consists of formulae such as "Good Morning," "Thank you for being here today," "Thank you for the opportunity to speak here at…" etc.
In many situations the speaker will introduce her/himself and/or will address a certain number of people present and/or absent with or without their names and full titles. Apart from getting the names and titles right, it is also of utmost importance not to confuse them. Hence, it is very important to pay close attention to what the speaker is saying and to also note down if s/he is introducing her/himself or referring to other people present. Especially when dealing with languages with names which do not allow for easy gender recognition, it is useful to also note down the gender of a person referred to so as not to mistakenly address somebody as a Mr. X when they are in fact a Ms X.

Exclamations And Questions

Use question marks (?) and exclamation marks (!) to mark whether a speaker is asking a direct and/or indirect question or making an exclamation. Omitting these will make your interpretation of the speech incomplete and could even lead to complete distortion and misunderstanding of what is being said.
Think, for example, about the differences below and how the oral representation of the full stop (.) question mark (?) and exclamation mark (!) influence the meaning of what is being said:

- He did it.
- He did it?
- He did it!

As it is sometimes not always possible to simply remember from the context of your notes which of the three options the speaker used, it is important when necessary to emphasise the type of speech. This is especially true if a speech event is too long to rely on your memory alone.

Extraordinary Information

Allow for the unexpected! You might hear information that does not fall into any of the above categories but cannot be considered part of the main idea either. This is, however, important information which nevertheless has to be accounted for. This might involve making a note to yourself that, for example, at one point of the speech the speaker started crying or swearing profusely, that what was being said was incomprehensible or repeated several times, or that someone else began speaking. These are all events which you have to account for in your interpretation of the original speech event. Always remember: you are not supposed to *clean up* what you are hearing, you are only meant to transport it from the speaker to the listener.

Links

Note down all those parts of speech which connect ideas and concepts, i.e. all link words such as because, and, so, or, if, etc.
This will help you in connecting the pieces of information on your note pad and makes for a clearly arranged set of information that is easily accessible for your eye at the time of interpretation. Apart from organising and structuring your 'written' version of the speech event, it also further draws your attention to these link words. The simple fact that the speaker used them in the original speech event is evidence of their importance in the structure of that event, as without them, any speech event would simply be an incoherent string of ideas.

What To Write In The Large Sections On Your Pages

- Each section is one separate point / thought / sentence

Section 1	Section 2
	He ran from the crime scene toward the car.
Then	**he seemed to struggle with the lock on the car door.**
Suddenly	**the door did open.**
Once	**he got into the car he sped off.**
Then	**I no longer saw him.**

The Notepad

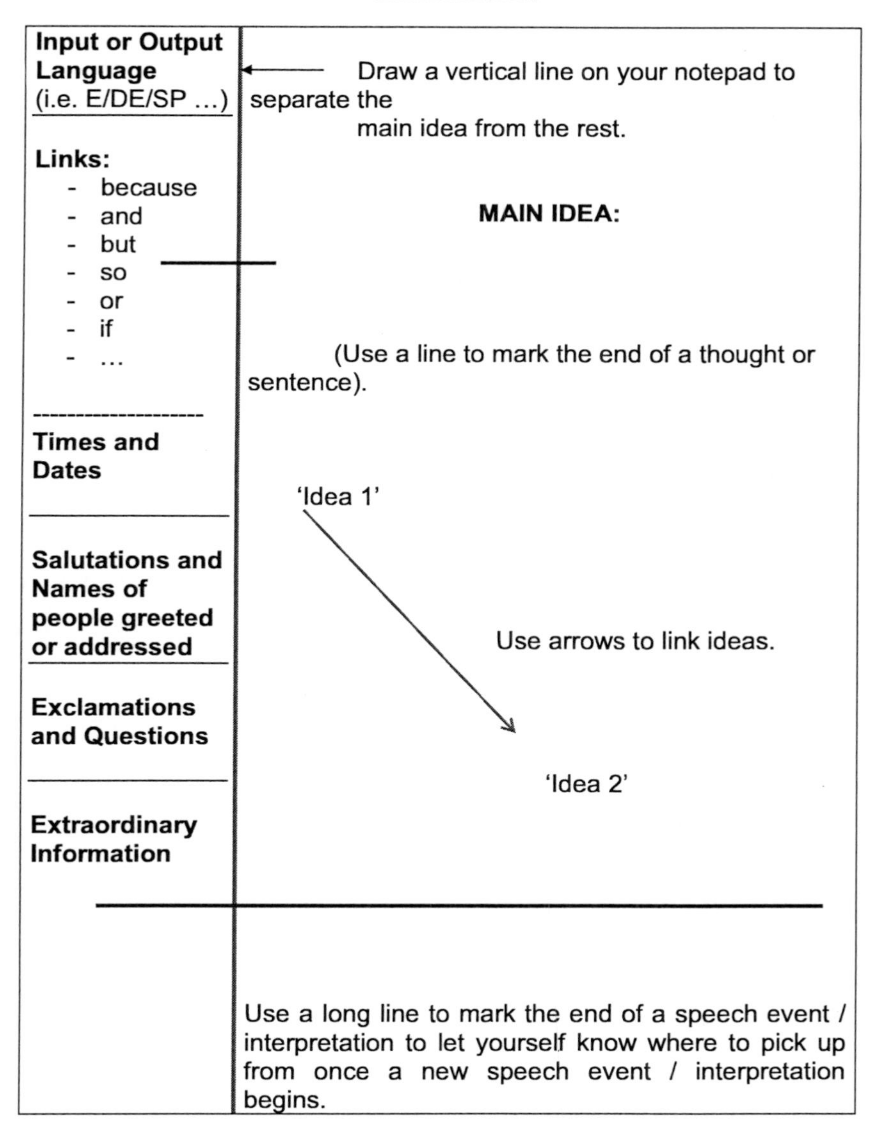
Input or Output Language
(i.e. E/DE/SP ...)
Draw a vertical line on your notepad to separate the main idea from the rest.
Links:
- because
- and
- but
- so
- or
- if
- ...
MAIN IDEA:
(Use a line to mark the end of a thought or sentence).
Times and Dates
'Idea 1'
Salutations and Names of people greeted or addressed
Use arrows to link ideas.
Exclamations and Questions
'Idea 2'
Extraordinary Information
Use a long line to mark the end of a speech event / interpretation to let yourself know where to pick up from once a new speech event / interpretation begins.

Main Idea

Use the bigger section of your notepad to note down the main idea of what is being said. Do remember that it is not necessary to write down everything the speaker says. You are not meant to make a word for word translation; your task is to transfer what is said from one language into the other. Hence, it is sufficient to note down the main idea in a way that will help you trigger your memory at the time of interpretation enabling you to recall the necessary information. Most speeches are not a random string of pieces of information, but are rather like a story with interconnected and linked pieces of information in a certain sequence. Noting down a condensed version connected with, e.g. arrows or short link words is sufficient to enable you to reconstruct a coherent and truthful version at the time of interpreting.

Noting down information in itself is an important process. It involves understanding what is being said, processing it, stripping it down to the core, noting down that core while, at the same time, still allowing for enough information to trigger your memory. Simply by going through this very process, you are memorising a substantial part of the incoming information which then enables you to concentrate more on the subtleties and the fine-tuning of your interpretation.

Note-taking is a very personal process and will only develop into a useful tool through trial-and-error. You should allocate some time and be prepared for a lot of wasted paper containing unintelligible scribbling that seems to make no sense at all at the time of interpreting before you eventually work out a system that works for you. Once you have mastered it, however, note-taking will make for a reliable tool whenever you are booked for an assignment that requires you to interpret consecutively.

And, believe it or not, the longer you practise note-taking, the longer the periods of time will become after which you can still reproduce a speech from your own notes. In addition your memory will also begin to improve – effectively minimising the volume of notes which you will need to take.

How Do You Develop Your Own Set Of Symbols For Note-Taking?

- Although every interpreter has to develop their own set of symbols there are some basic principles and guidelines that can be applied to make the process easier.

- These guidelines are not binding, but if you bear them in mind when designing your symbols they can prove to be quite helpful.

Criteria For Developing Your Own Symbols

- Wherever possible one symbol should be used for a whole idea. For example when preparing for an assignment on drugs it is not essential to have a separate symbol for every type of drug. The best approach is to have one symbol which you can use for drugs in general and then determine which type of drug you are referring to by adding a letter. The process of using symbols should not be made unnecessarily difficult by requiring you to learn a multitude of new symbols almost as if you were learning another language,
  e.g.

Drugs (first letter of the word)

Heroin (as above with H for Heroin)

Cannabis (as above with C for Cannabis)

Amphetamines (as above with A for Amphetamines)

- The less language-bound a symbol is the better. This is especially true when your source language is very different to your target language e.g. where there is a different script, e.g.

Person, human being		(stick man)
Transport, vehicle		(2 wheels on an axle)
Liquid		(droplet)
Country		(circle as on number plates)

- The symbol has to be convincing, it has to convey an image. This does not, however, mean that you have to be an artist to create symbols – this is also the reason why children are a very good help when creating symbols as they will always tend to draw things in a very simplified way, e.g.

Danger		(simplified sign as for dangerous goods)
Say	"	(speech marks)
Building		(two walls with a roof)
See		(simplified eye)

- The symbol can and should cover a wide range of similar terms, e.g.

Say, state, speak, inform etc.

Danger, peril, threat etc.

Human being, person, he, she

- Although you do require a broad range of symbols covering very different topics, it is counter-productive to have too many symbols – you are not meant to invent a new language, but to have an effective tool. Hence, you do not need a single symbol for every word but rather for word categories or families, e.g.

Human being, person

Old person

Injured / sick person

Dead person, murder victim

Baby

- So let's have a closer look at the symbol for human being. Before considering which symbol to use for a single human being, take a piece of paper and list as many words for human beings as you can think of such as man, child, mother, ill person etc. Then put them in relation to each other, e.g. group them according to age etc. Next take a step back and have a look at or create your basic symbol for a human being – make it as basic and simple as possible. Now put this basic symbol next to each of the terms on your list for human beings. Before creating a symbol for each of those terms, think about in how far it differs from your basic symbol, i.e. if your basic symbol for a human being is a stick man ( ) and you are looking for a symbol for an old age pensioner, one good idea would be to simply bend that person's back ( ) – this is visually effective, as you still see the person and by bending their back, indicate that that person is old as most of the elderly walk with a slightly bent back.

- Now let's have a look at extending symbols already in use by merging them with different symbols, thus creating completely new ones.
  Again, let's use the basic symbol for a human being ( ).
  Assuming you need a symbol for *a person needing asylum* – an asylum seeker. Taking a closer look at the term and its explanation, there are three aspects to it: a person ( ), asylum ( ) and wanting/needing something ( ).
  Noting down all three symbols in a row like this

would be very time and space consuming. A far better strategy is to combine all three symbols by merging them into one.
e.g.

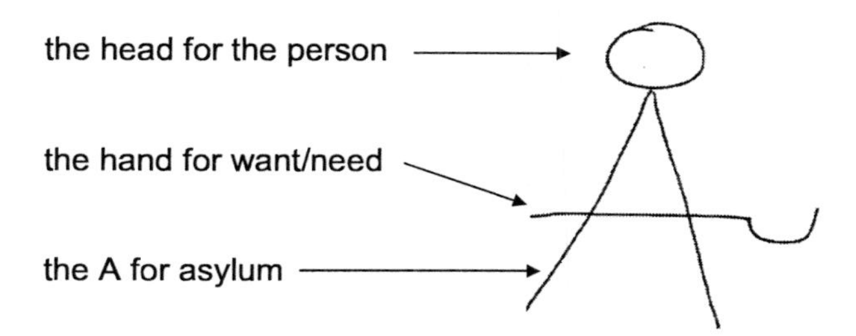

Note that the three individual symbols are truly merged, each giving up part of their own, fusing with the others, yet still recognizable.

This exercise can be applied to all of your symbols e.g.

Let's use another example with asylum:

Country

Asylum

Country of Asylum

Country of Origin / Home Country

Now let's look at a completely different topic:

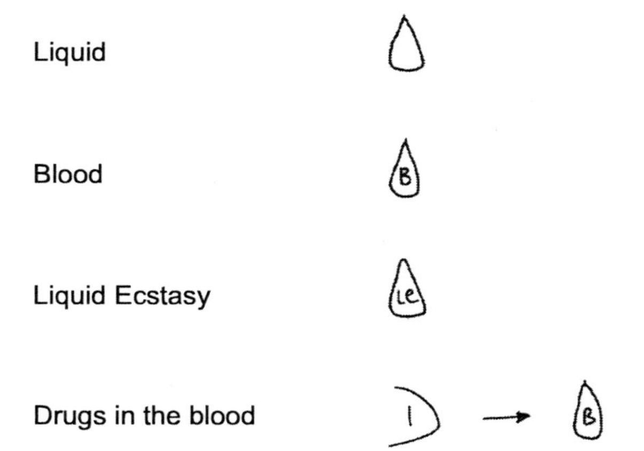

However, with some symbols, a true merging might not be possible. Here, you can simply write them close to each other to indicate to yourself that they belong together to form one concept or invent a completely new symbol.

- Arrows can be used to indicate various aspects. This saves the interpreter a lot of time when they do not have to write down a word or a whole expression but can simply use an arrow. Examples would be
    - To indicate an increase / growth etc.

The person's drug consumption increased

(Symbol for Drugs, symbol for human being and arrow to show increase)

- To indicate reduction / something becoming less

We were able to reduce security measures.

(Symbol for reduction, symbol of an umbrella for security/protection, and *m* for measures)

- To indicate movement e.g. a journey

He fled from his home country and travelled via France to the UK.

(Merge symbols for home and country, arrows indicating movement and respective country symbols with first letter of word in circle)

The defendant ran from the crime scene straight to his car.

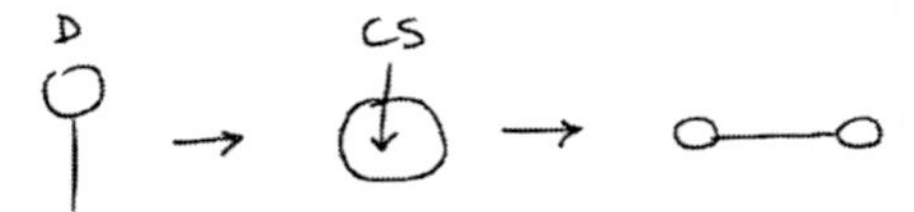

(Symbol for human being with *D* for defendant, arrows indicating movement, symbol for location i.e. arrow pointing at a place with *CS* for crime scene and symbol for car)

- To connect various elements

His crime was so serious that it made him a target in prison.

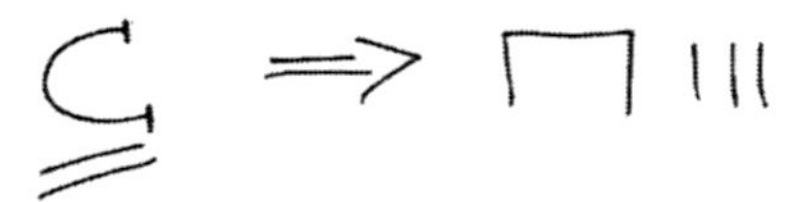

(Symbol for crime, underlining for level of seriousness, symbol for consequence, symbol for target/goal, symbol for prison)

She had a weak heart, which caused the fatal heart attack.

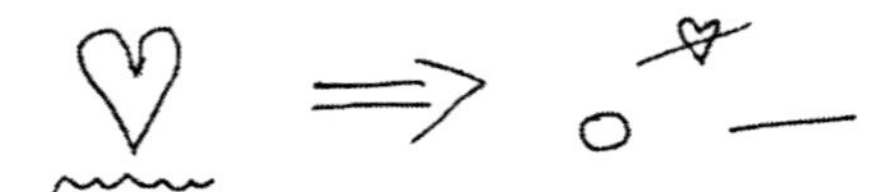

(symbol for heart with a wavy line to indicate weakness, symbol for consequence, symbol for dead person with crossed out heart indicating heart attack)

- Intensifying / Weakening

- Sometimes expressions or words need to be intensified or weakened. The words used to do this are extremely important and cannot ever be ignored in the interpretation, nevertheless it would be extremely time-consuming to have to write words such as *very*, *extremely* or *little* etc. This should therefore be avoided and a good way of emphasising or weakening is:

    - underlining with a straight line for emphasis, or two lines for even stronger emphasis,
      e.g.

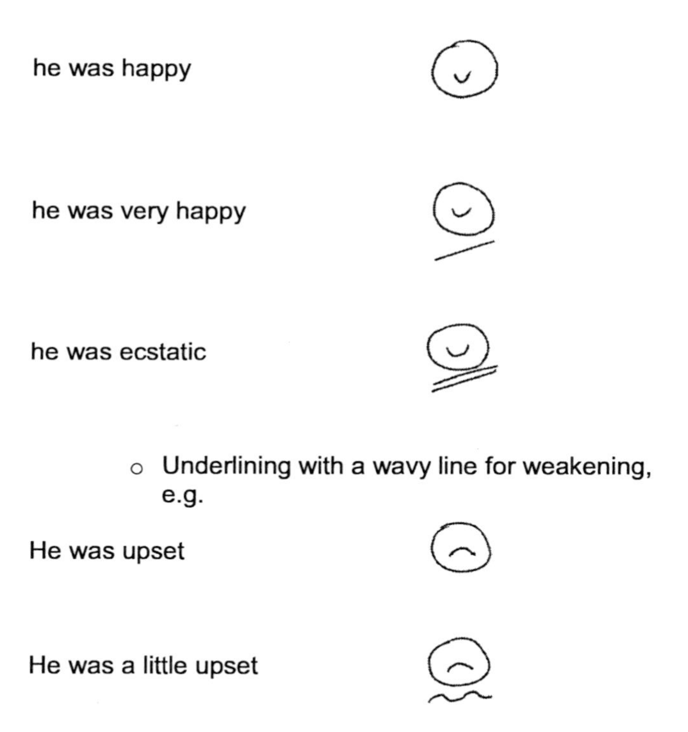

he was happy
he was very happy
he was ecstatic
Underlining with a wavy line for weakening, e.g.
He was upset
He was a little upset

- Abbreviations

  Abbreviations are often used instead of symbols. However, beware! If they are used, they have to be logical, comprehensible and not ambiguous in a situation where quick thinking and understanding are required. Good abbreviations are always those which are common knowledge or generally used, such as

United Nations	UN
Her Majesty's Prison Service	HMP
Crown Prosecution Service	CPS
Community Psychiatric Nurse	CPN

However, dangerous cases of abbreviation are for example:

dif where you want to use the abbreviation to mean *difficult*. This is a danger as *dif* could also mean *different*, *diffuse* etc.

Such abbreviations **do not work**!

- Language-bound symbols are often used where the words are similar in both languages. They are often abbreviations or first letters of words, for example:

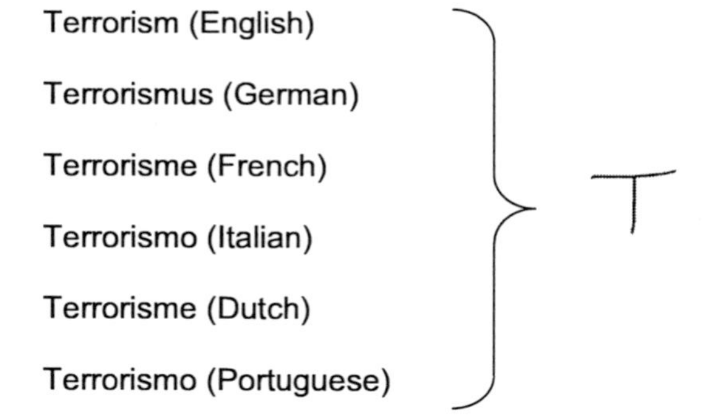

- Where the interpreter decides to use one or the other language for some language-bound symbols. Here it is important that the symbol is always used only in the one language,
  e.g.

  PO = Police Officer

  (always use English only if you have decided to use the English rather than the other language term which may be a different abbreviation)

- Crossing Out for negation:
  - When wishing to negate a word the easiest approach is to cross out the word. It is much faster than writing words such as *not* or *didn't*,
    e.g.

He saw

(Symbol for eye)

He did not see

He drank

(Symbol of a glass)

He did not drink

She walked

(Symbol of a pair of legs with feet for walking)

She did not walk 

- Crossing out to indicate the opposite meaning of a word, e.g.

Legal 

(Symbol of simplified scales as held by the statue of Justice)

Illegal 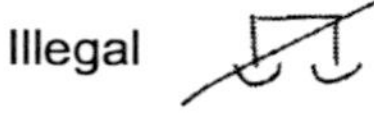

Drunk 

(Symbol for a full glass)

Sober 

- There are various systems to indicate the plural of a term. In the English language the plural is usually indicated by an *s* on the end of the word. This can also be used to indicate the plural of a symbol, e.g.

person 

(stick man drawing – simplified with only head and body)

people

animal

(stick animal drawing – simplified with only two legs)

animals

Input Or Output Language:

Anyone who has ever had a conversation with a group of people where more than one language was involved knows that it is easy to confuse those languages used in the discussion. Therefore making a note of either the language you are hearing or the language you will be interpreting into is a useful tool. You will find that not having to remember which language to use will alleviate the pressure somewhat. This is particularly applicable when interpreting in difficult or emotionally draining circumstances.
So, for example, use the top left corner to note *EN* if you want to remind yourself that what you heard was in English and you have to speak in the other language.

Note-Taking Made Easy – Let's Recap:

Let's just recap what we know about the main tools of the Consecutive Interpreter, namely the notepad and a functioning set of symbols.

The notepad is far more than just an A5 pad of paper – it is your best possible aid and memory trigger. It is the drawing board on which you can simplify complicated ideas voiced by the speaker. It provides the blueprint of what you are going to say. It calms your nerves as it provides you with the security of knowing that you do not have to remember a seemingly endless stream of information while, at the same time, trying to think about just how to convey that information in the other language. And, last but not least, it gives you something to simply hold on to!

The Consecutive Interpreter's other main tool is the set of functioning symbols. These symbols help you note down complex and weighty information in a simplified and language-independent manner. This then leaves enough time in which to concentrate on actually listening to the speaker and subsequently processing what is being said. This process is vital in being able to provide the listener with a useful interpretation.
Not only will your symbols save writing time, they will allow you to focus your mind on the ongoing speech without the fear of having missed or forgotten any of that previous information.

While developing functioning symbols may initially seem to be confusing and complicated, it is a process that will ultimately pay great dividends. This is because not only will you be able to note down a lot more basic information which will in turn give you the time to pay more attention to the subtleties of what is being said (e.g. little utterances, emotions of the speaker, secondary information and asides etc.), but also because you will have further developed and extended your vocabulary. In addition, your understanding of many more important concepts will have developed and you will undoubtedly have honed your comprehension skills.

CHAPTER 5

NOTE-TAKING – TRAINING OVER, LET'S GET STARTED!

Now that you understand the theory of note-taking and the basic ideas for creating your own symbols, let's have a look at how it works in practice.

You will see below a short piece of realistic court opening address from a fictitious interpreting assignment, which is ultimately going to be rendered consecutively.

- First read the text and look for all the important terms / concepts / ideas for which you think you may need to create a symbol.

Members of the Jury, you have here before you three defendants accused of kidnapping and actual bodily harm. It is my task and my team's task to prove to you beyond reasonable doubt that the incident involving the victim Mr. Kasanowski took place in the exact way it is spelt out in the charges in the indictment. You must never forget that until the Prosecution has proven the defendants' guilt you have to presume them innocent. Now let me outline the facts of the case.

On the 20th September 2007 Mr Kasanowski was walking home from work the usual way along Smithy Lane past Blakemere Park. Initially he did not become aware of the man that was following him on foot. After he had passed the park, he noticed that someone walking behind him was coming closer and closer.

Shortly after, he noticed a car driving very slowly alongside him. He later described this car as a black Mercedes SLK Convertible with it's roof open. This type of car was later identified as belonging to one of the three defendants, namely Mr Bjørnssen.

These are terms the authors would have highlighted:

Members of the **Jury**, you have here before you **three** defendants accused of **kidnapping** and **actual bodily harm**. It is my task and my team's task to **prove** to you **beyond reasonable doubt** that the incident involving the victim **Mr. Kasanowski** took place in the exact way it is spelt out in the **charges** in the **indictment**. You must never forget that until the **Prosecution** has proven the defendants' **guilt** you have to presume them **innocent**. Now let me outline the **facts** of the **case**.

On the **20th September 2007** Mr Kasanowski was walking home from work the usual way along **Smithy Lane** past **Blakemere Park**. Initially he did **not** become **aware** of the **man** that was **following** him on foot. After he had **passed the park**, he noticed that **someone** walking behind him was **coming closer** and closer.

Shortly after, he noticed a **car** driving very **slowly alongside** him. He **later** described this car as a **black Mercedes SLK Convertible** with its **roof open**. This type of car was later identified as **belonging** to one of the three **defendants**, namely **Mr Bjørnssen**.

- Now spend some time developing symbols for the highlighted terms, remembering the criteria for developing symbols outlined earlier in this book.

- Then spend some time trying to retain / remember the symbols you have developed and practise jotting them down quickly and legibly, possibly even improving them.

- Now take a break of at least half an hour during which you do not look at or even think about the text, its content or the symbols you have just developed.

- After your break find someone to read out the text to you, at a normal speaking pace, while you try to take notes.

- Then repeat the content of the text from your notes whilst your practising partner checks your delivery for

    - Accuracy
    - Completeness
    - Presentation
    - Style
    - Fluency

- Now encourage your practising partner to give you honest and constructive criticism and feedback on the above five criteria.

- Now go through your notes and check how many of the symbols which you developed earlier you have actually used.

- Spend some time thinking about why you used some of them but not others and about any other problems you encountered.

1. Was the symbol too detailed?
2. Was the symbol too difficult to remember?
3. Did you think of something better that worked on the spur of the moment?
4. Did you think of something that seemed a good idea on the spur of the moment, but could not remember it when you were rendering the speech?
5. Were there sections of your notes which you were unable to read at all?
6. Did you use the prepared symbols but fail to connect them correctly in order for them to make sense?
7. Did you jot down certain information but find that you had not listened to the speaker?
8. Did you spend too much time thinking about the symbols whilst writing them?
9. Did you feel very uncomfortable and/or nervous presenting to your practising partner (public speaking)?

Let's look at some solutions to the above problems:

1. **Was the symbol too detailed?**

   It is always worthwhile developing a symbol and then taking a separate look at it and downsizing or simplifying it as a next step. This process sometimes happens long after you first developed the symbol, which is absolutely fine.

2. **Was the symbol too difficult to remember?**

   If that was the case you need to modify or change the symbol you have been using.

3. **Did you think of something better that worked on the spur of the moment?**

   Often the spontaneous ideas / inventions / creations are the best – so stick with them.

4. **Did you think of something that seemed a good idea on the spur of the moment, but could not remember it when you were rendering the speech?**

   Either disregard them instantly or save them to go back to at a later stage to re-test them – this sometimes works once you have spent more time working on symbols.

5. **Could you not read some of your notes at all?**

   It is important not to expect too much from your first few attempts at practising, and legibility will improve with continuous practice. Reading your notes becomes easier as you start using them more. Don't forget the less you jot down, the more time you have to write the symbols down clearly and legibly.

6. **Did you use the prepared symbols but fail to connect them correctly in order for them to make sense?**
   Go back to the section on links and linking words, and also the use of linkwords as a structuring tool on your page. In addition to this you might want to work on text comprehension exercises to speed up your information processing abilities.

7. **Did you jot down certain information but find that you had not listened to the speaker?**
   The best approach to this problem is to concentrate on split attention and memory skills improvement. Please refer to the section on memory skills in this book.

8. **Did you spend too much time thinking about the symbols whilst writing them?**
   You have no other choice – practise recalling and writing them down over and over again! Also check if they actually work for you.

9. **Did you feel very uncomfortable and/or nervous presenting to your practising partner (public speaking)?**
   Think about why you felt uncomfortable; was it because you were actually having to perform in front of somebody else instead of the mirror or an empty room, or was it because you still require more time to practise and hone your skills to a level at which you feel competent and confident in your ability to act as an interpreter.

CHAPTER 6

NOTE-TAKING EXERCISES

EXERCISE: Develop functioning symbols for the following terms.

SYMBOL	ENGLISH	OTHER LANGUAGE
	court	
	police	
	health	
	person	
	accident	
	danger	
	police station	
	hospital	
	weapon	
	blood	
	Social Services	
	water	

	interpreter	
	hear	
	walk	
	ambulance	
	thought	
	car	
	lorry	
	protection	
	help	

(See Appendix, pages 151-153 for possible solutions. Please remember that you are not bound by these possible solutions. If you have found a better symbol that works for you, then go ahead and use it.)

Note-Taking Exercises

When practising your note-taking skills, it is important to concentrate not only on inventing symbols, but to also work on fluency and vocabulary, i.e. the amount of symbols you use.

As with every skill, note-taking needs to be practised on a frequent basis – the more you practise, the easier the process will become, eventually enabling you to note down complex information without having to think about it.

Exercises to do on your own

1. One good way of practising your note-taking skills is to force yourself not to write out longhand things such as your shopping list or your *To-Do* list, but to put it on paper in symbol form. As the information contained is relatively straight forward and the lists are rather short, this is a simple and repetitive, yet still effective, way of memorizing and extending your symbols.

2. You can also use a newspaper article or any other written document to practise note-taking. Read through the entire document once and highlight the most important words. Remember not only nouns and verbs are important words. Adjectives such as *sad*, *small* etc. can change the meaning of a sentence. Once you have located these terms try to develop symbols for these.

3. Another useful exercise is transcription. Use any informative written text of at least 500 words (excerpts from books, magazines, newspapers, journals etc.) and ensure that, with time, the information contained in them becomes gradually more complex and the texts longer, gradually changing from topics that you are interested in to topics related to Public Service Interpreting. Read through the entire text to gain a general understanding of the context. Then go back to the beginning of the text and after reading the first sentence again, note it down while actively thinking about which

parts are the key information. Justify everything you put on your note pad. Once you have finished noting down the entire text sentence by sentence, put away the original and re-write the text from your notes. Then compare the original text and your own written version paying special attention to those pieces of information retrieved from your notes and those pieces retrieved from your memory triggered by the notes themselves. This will further enable you to minimize the amount of information you actually have to put down on your note pad and to achieve a better structure of that information which you do have to note down.

4. A further very effective exercise is to listen to a programme on the radio or television and to take notes of what you hear while taping or video recording the programme at the same time. Once the programme is finished or you feel you have taken notes for sufficient time, take a few minutes to read through your work. Then, return to the first page and formulate the first sentence in your head. Then read out your notes aloud making sure you are performing as if in a real life interpreting situation (i.e. act professionally, do not make comments, do not go back to the beginning if you made a mistake, ensure you sound confident). Once finished, rewind the taped or recorded programme and listen to it while going through your notes. As you do this, pay attention to any omissions you made, information you invented and/ or missed out. In order for this exercise to be effective, you should repeat it as often as possible. While doing so, pay special attention to any pattern developing with regard to repetitive mistakes such as omissions, getting relations between concepts/thoughts wrong, having numbers wrong, etc. These are the areas you will have to concentrate on with further exercise or even by simply altering your symbol or note-taking technique.

Exercises to do in groups (of two or more)

The early stages of note-taking practise can be very disillusioning. It is much more fun to practice together – always bearing in mind that other people's symbols may not work for you, but may provide inspiration.

1. As before, use a newspaper article or any other written document to practise note-taking in a group. Read through the entire document once and highlight the most important words. Remember not only nouns and verbs are important words e.g. adjectives such as *sad*, *small* etc. can change the meaning of a sentence. This part of the exercise can be prepared by all group members in advance and once you meet start discussing the terms. This is a fun exercise which will also inspire you.

2. Now using the same document, select a speaker who will read out the text to the other group members who try to note it down in symbols as much as possible. The speaker should remember not to make the interventions too short even if some of the group members are struggling initially. Then the speaker chooses one group member to repeat the words read in the same language.

3. Same as exercise number two but if you have one or several practising partners who speak English and the same foreign language, then you can render the words read out by the speaker in the other language.

4. Meet as a group (you do not have to speak the same other language) and discuss your areas of specialism which do not need to be related to interpreting e.g. one of you plays an instrument. Then analyse whether this specialism uses any subject- specific symbols (e.g. musical notes). Discuss how you could use or modify these to suit your needs.

CHAPTER 7

SAMPLES OF SYMBOLS IN CATEGORIES

Police (1)

SYMBOL	ENGLISH	EXPLANATION
P	police	Using first letter of the word
	police officer	Using first letters of words and head for human being
	police station	Using first letter of word and roof for building
	police car	Using first letter of word and wheels for vehicle
	police force	Using first letter of word and circle to show entirety
TAU	Tactical Aid Unit	An initialism
	crime	Using first letter of word with a vertical line at both ends to differentiate the C for Crime from the C for Court
	crime prevention	Symbol for crime and no entry sign from traffic signs

Police (2)

SYMBOL	ENGLISH	EXPLANATION
	victim	A person lying down
	offender	C for crime with a head to show it is a person
	witness	A person who has seen something => eye in the head
	taped interview	An audio tape and the speech marks for speaking
	suspect	First letter of word and head for person
	statement	Speech marks for the spoken word on a sheet of paper
	custody	Using first letter of the word and bars to show imprisonment
	custody suite	Symbol for custody adding the symbol for building

Police (3)

SYMBOL	ENGLISH	EXPLANATION
	Custody Sergeant	Symbol for custody and symbol for police officer
	arresting officer	Using first letters of words and head for human being
	interviewing officer	Using first letters of words and head for human being
	cell	Bars from window of cell
	charge	Large exclamation mark (not ! as this is used for something else)
	charge sheet	Symbol for charge and symbol for a sheet of paper
	rights	Symbol used for laws/articles of law in some languages
	entitlements	Using first letter but writing it as a large curved E, so it cannot be mistaken for a normal E

Police (4)

SYMBOL	ENGLISH	EXPLANATION
	caution	Using first letter of the word but with an exclamation mark
	swab	The item used to take a swab from someone's mouth
	breathaliser test	Mouth of a person with a pipe coming out of it (the part of the test machine you have to breath into)
DNA	DNA	An initialism
	duty solicitor	For all types of legal professionals we use the first letter of their name and the wig (even though not all of them wear a wig!) and d for duty
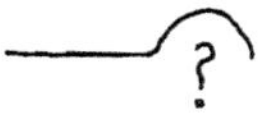	search	Symbol for a hand taking something and in the hand the question mark for searching
	warrant	Symbol for sheet of paper and W for warrant
	search warrant	Symbol for warrant and question mark for search

Courts (1)

SYMBOL	ENGLISH	EXPLANATION
	court	Using first letter of word and roof for building
	judge	Using first letter of word and wig for legal professional
	jury	A jury consists of 12 people => 12 and symbol for person
	witness box	Symbol for a simplified bench with first letter of word
	dock	Symbol for a simplified bench with first letter of word
	defendant	Symbol for defendant
	accused	Symbol for bench and arrow pointing to the accused
	usher	First letter of symbol and head for human being

Courts (2)

SYMBOL	ENGLISH	EXPLANATION
	indictment	Symbol for sheet of paper with i for indictment
	summons	Symbol for court and an arrow to show they have to go to court
	verdict	A sheet of paper with a tick
	sentence	Symbol for verdict with an arrow going up/out
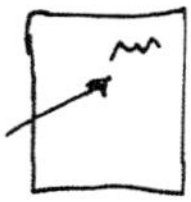	count	Symbol for sheet of paper with a scribble for writing on it for the count that would be written on it
QC	Queen's Counsel (QC)	An initialism
	solicitor	Using first letter of word and wig for legal professional
	barrister	Using first letter of word and wig for legal professional

Courts (3)

SYMBOL	ENGLISH	EXPLANATION
LA	legal adviser	Symbol for legal professional and first letters of words
£	fine	Symbol for money and an arrow showing the money going out
	background	Lines which children use when filling in the background of a picture
H	holding cells	Bars for prison cell with an H for holding
	consultation	Two people talking to each other (speech marks for talking)
Ch	chambers	First two letters of word and roof for building
	plead	Speech marks and arrow to show pleading
	date	I for time line with a vertical line under it to mean date

Courts (4)

SYMBOL	ENGLISH	EXPLANATION
g.	guilty	Using first letter of word in lower case and full stop to differentiate it from other words starting with g
~~g.~~	not guilty	Symbol for guilty, crossed out
£ |||	bail	Symbol for money and symbol for prison
	oath	Speech marks in a circle underlined twice for oath
	affirmation	Speech marks in a circle underlined once for affirmation
→ ^C	attend court	Symbol for court and arrow showing process of going to court
CPS	Crown Prosecution Service	An initialism
WST	Witness Support Team	An initialism

Probation Service (1)

SYMBOL	ENGLISH	EXPLANATION
	probation	Symbol for prison with and arrow through it to show person coming out of prison
	Probation Officer	Symbol for probation with head for human being
	Probation Service	Symbol for probation and first letter of second word
	alcohol education course	Special C with long tail for all courses, glass for alcohol and ed for education
	bail hostel	Symbol for prison but wavy underlining to indicate not quite prison
	community sentence	Symbol for sheet of paper with first letters of words on it
CRO	community rehabilitation order	An initialism
ASBO	Anti-social Behaviour Order	An acronym

Probation Service (2)

SYMBOL	ENGLISH	EXPLANATION
	curfew	Symbol for prison but combined with the symbol for home
	electronic tagging	Symbol for electronic/ electric and leg with tag on it
	custodial sentence	Symbol for prison and symbol for sentence
	low risk offender	Symbol for criminal with a wavy line
NPS	National Probation Service	An initialism
PB	Parole Board	An initialism
r'hab	rehabilitation	Using the word but in a shortened form
lic	licence	Symbol for sheet of paper with first three letters of word

Probation (3)

SYMBOL	ENGLISH	EXPLANATION
CRB	criminal record	Symbol for sheet of paper and acronym for Criminal Records Bureau
CRB ?	CRB check	Symbol for criminal record and question mark for check/search
+	previous good character	Person with + for good and arrow pointing back to indicate previous
	crime reduction	Symbol for crime and arrow pointing downwards for reduction
	deterrence	Frightened looking face to show the person is deterred
£	reparation	Payment of money
rda	risk and dangerousness assessment	Using first letters of words
	protection of public	Symbol for an umbrella for protection and symbol of person on half circle for public

Probation Service (4)

SYMBOL	ENGLISH	EXPLANATION
	paid work	Alpha symbol chosen for work and smiley face for being paid
	unpaid work	Symbol for work and miserable face to show it is unpaid
SSO	suspended sentence order	Symbol for sheet of paper with first letters of words
	attendance centre	Symbol for building with person in it
D r'hab	drug rehabilitation	Symbol for drugs and symbol for rehabilitation
	loss of job	Symbol for work crossed out to show loss
[ ]	restrictions	Square brackets to indicate restriction
[V&t]	visa and travel restrictions	Symbol for restriction and first letters of both words

H.M. Prison Service (1)

SYMBOL	ENGLISH	EXPLANATION
HMP	Her Majesty's Prison Service	An initialism
	prison	Bars on windows in prison
	prison officer	Symbol for prison with head for human being
	governor	Symbol for prison, first letter of word with head for human being
	wing	Symbol for prison and symbol for wings (of a bird)
	on remand	Prison symbol with person on left hand bar (before trial)
	in prison	Prison symbol with person on middle bar (in prison without specification)
	lifer	Prison symbol with person on right bar (sentenced to life)

H.M. Prison Service (2)

SYMBOL	ENGLISH	EXPLANATION
	reception	Symbol for chair in front of reception desk
	handcuffs	Symbol for open handcuffs
	cell search	Symbol for prison and question mark for search
	open prison	Symbol for prison and the roof upside down to show it is open
	closed prison	Symbol for prison and two roofs to show it is closed
	high security prison	Symbol for prison with exclamation mark to show high level of security
	remand centre	Symbol for remand and roof to show building
YOI	Young Offenders Institution	An initialism

H.M. Prison Service (3)

SYMBOL	ENGLISH	EXPLANATION
Cat A	Category A Prison (A-D)	First three letters of word and letter A to D depending on category
	control and restraint	Symbol for handcuffs and first letters of words
R!	place on report	Letter R with speech marks in it as symbol for report and exclamation mark for placing on
	loss of privileges	Symbol for hand taking away the privileges and sad face
	self harm	Symbol for person lying down = injured, with arrow coming out of head
	suicide	Symbol for person without head = dead, with arrow coming out of head
	restraint	Symbol for handcuffs with first letter of word
	duties	Symbol for hand with exclamation mark to show it has to be done

H.M. Prison Service (4)

SYMBOL	ENGLISH	EXPLANATION
X mgt	incident management	X for incident and mgt as an abbreviation for management
trl	terrorist response levels	Using first letters of the words
[handwritten symbol]	convicted	Symbol for sheet of paper with symbol for verdict and miserable face
adj))	adjudication hearing	First three letters of first word and symbol for ear for hearing
ed [handwritten symbol]	training facilities	Symbol for training which is ed (from education) and symbol for roof for facilities
[handwritten symbol]	visitors' centre	Symbol of coffee cup for visit and symbol for roof for centre
[handwritten symbol]	canteen	Symbol for knife and fork
[handwritten symbol]	prison visit	Symbol for prison and symbol for visit (a coffee cup)

Offences (1)

SYMBOL	ENGLISH	EXPLANATION
	money laundering	Symbol for two hands dealing with money
	assault	A fist hitting a head
	murder	Symbol for a dead body with a knife above it
	burglary	A hand reaching into a house
	theft	A hand with the first letter of word under it
	robbery	A hand with the first letter of word under it
	armed robbery	A hand with the first letter of word under it and a weapon above it to show it was armed
	fraud	C for crime with hand at the end of it and first letter of word

Offences (2)

SYMBOL	ENGLISH	EXPLANATION
TWOC	taking without owner's consent	An acronym
	manslaughter	Symbol for murder with a wavy line to say not quite murder
	ID theft	Symbol for hand taking with ID under it, to show the identity is being taken
	sex	Two people lying on top of each other
	sexual assault	Symbol for sex with A for assault
	rape	Symbol for sex with R for rape
	sexual harassment	Symbol for sex with H for harassment
	stalking	Symbol for person with a pair of legs behind them which are following them

Offences (3)

SYMBOL	ENGLISH	EXPLANATION
	race	First letter of the word in capitals with circle in it
	racially aggravated	Symbol for race underlined twice to show aggravation
	kidnapping	Symbol of hand taking a person
 C £	blackmail	C for crime with hand taking money
 C £	bribery	C for crime with hand giving money
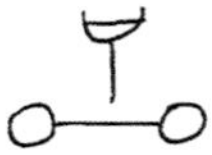	drink driving	Symbol for vehicle with symbol for alcohol
ABH	Actual Bodily Harm	An initialism
GBH	Grievous Bodily Harm	An initialism

Offences (4)

SYMBOL	ENGLISH	EXPLANATION
	negligence	Hand which is doing something with wavy line to show it is not done properly
	conspiracy	Symbol for speaking in round brackets to show secrecy
	wounding	Round W to differentiate it from other words starting with W
	possession of weapons	Symbol for hand holding a weapon
	prostitution	Symbol for sex and money inside to show payment for sex
	soliciting	Symbol for sex and question mark to show searching for customers
	kerb crawling	Symbol for sex and question mark outside to show person searching for prostitute
	pimping	Symbol for hand taking the proceeds from sex (from the prostitute)

Drugs (1)

SYMBOL	ENGLISH	EXPLANATION
	drugs	First letter of word and small s for plural
	drug dealer	Symbol for drugs and head for human being on top
	drug user	Symbol for drugs with head for human being inside
	drug addict	Symbol for drug user with head underlined to show addiction
	acquisitory crime	Symbol for crime and hand to show taking
	snorting	A nose snorting a line (e.g. of cocaine)
	sniffing	A nose sniffing fumes (e.g. of glue)
	inject	A syringe going into skin

Drugs (2)

SYMBOL	ENGLISH	EXPLANATION
	needle	Part of the syringe
	overdose	Symbol for dead person and syringe
	syringe	A syringe
	smoke	A smoking cigarette
C	cannabis	Symbol for drugs with a C for cannabis
H	heroin	Symbol for drugs with a H for heroin
Cr	crack	Symbol for drugs with a Cr for crack
Co	cocaine	Symbol for drugs with a Co for cocaine

Drugs (3)

SYMBOL	ENGLISH	EXPLANATION
	crack cocaine	Symbol for drugs with a Cr for crack and Co for Cocaine
	liquid ecstasy	Symbol for drugs with a LE for liquid ecstasy
	class of drug (A,B,C)	Symbol for drugs with first letter of class in brackets
	drug rehabilitation	Symbol for drug and symbol for rehabilitation
	alcohol abuse	Symbol for alcohol and a fuzzy head (how you feel after abuse of any kind)
	mandatory drugs test	Exclamation mark for mandatory, the test tube for test and symbol for drugs inside it
	blood specimen	Symbol of a droplet for any liquid with a B inside it for blood and the swab/ specimen symbol
	urine specimen	As above but with a U for urine

Drugs (4)

SYMBOL	ENGLISH	EXPLANATION
	impairment test	Symbol for test and a head with a furrowed brow for impairment
HIV	HIV	An initialism
Hep	Hepatitis	First three letters of word (commonly used abbreviation)
	glazed eyes	Symbol for eyes with a distorted pupil
	high	Symbol for a head on top of a cloud
	withdrawal symptoms	Face with downturned eyes and mouth
	crack house	Symbol for crack with roof for building
r'hab	rehabilitation	Symbol for rehabilitation

Immigration (1)

SYMBOL	ENGLISH	EXPLANATION
	immigration	Two lower case letters i to differentiate from other words starting with i
	asylum	A large a with a line going across and beyond the letter
	asylum seeker	Symbol for asylum with hand for seeking and head for human being
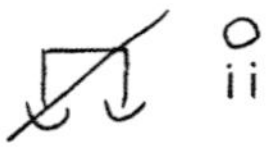	illegal immigrant	Symbol for illegal and symbol for immigration with head for human being
	country of origin	Symbol for country with roof to indicate home
	country of asylum	Symbol for country and symbol for asylum
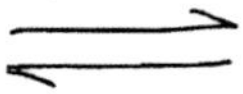	trafficking	Two half arrows showing something moving back and forth
	passport	Using two of the letters in the word

Immigration (2)

SYMBOL	ENGLISH	EXPLANATION
	interview	Symbol for sheet of paper with i and speech marks for interview
	appeal	A person shouting (mouth and exclamation mark), showing they are against it
	application	Symbol for sheet of paper and first two letters of word
ASU	Asylum Screening Unit	An initialism
	adjudicator	Symbol for legal professional with first letter of word
	removal	A hand with arrow facing away
	family relations	Symbol for relationship (two intertwined rings) with an F for family
	cultural background	First two letters of word cultural and symbol for background

Immigration (3)

SYMBOL	ENGLISH	EXPLANATION
	religious background	Using first letter of word and symbol for background
	immigration solicitor	Using symbol for immigration and symbol for solicitor
	torture	Sword/knife with blood droplets
	refugee	Using first letter of word in lower case with head for human being and arrow showing flight
	homeless	Symbol for house/home crossed out
	unaccompanied minors	Symbol for child with crossed out symbol for adult
	case work	Symbol for two sheets of paper with an s for plural
	politics	Pi (Greek letter)

Immigration (4)

SYMBOL	ENGLISH	EXPLANATION
HO	Home Office	An initialism
ii O	immigration officer	Symbol for immigration and O for officer – head can be added for human being
	grant asylum	Symbol of a hand giving/granting and symbol for asylum
	torturer	Symbol for torture with head for human being a handle-end to show it is the torturer
	victim of torture	Symbol for torture with head for human being at end of sword to show victim
	religious persecution	Symbol for eye and symbol for religion
	detention centre	Symbol for detention and roof for building

Tribunals (1)

SYMBOL	ENGLISH	EXPLANATION
	tribunal	Using first letter of word and roof for building
	adjudicator	Symbol for legal professional and symbol for tribunal
	applicant	Symbol for application and head for human being
	Industrial Tribunal	Symbol for tribunal and i for industrial
	employment, work	Based on German word for work which starts with A and was turned into alpha
	Employment Tribunal	Symbol for work and symbol for tribunal
	hearing	Symbol of an ear
	hearing date	Symbol for hearing and symbol for date

Tribunals (2)

SYMBOL	ENGLISH	EXPLANATION
TEA	Tribunals and Enquiries Act	First letters of first three words and symbol for law
	dismissal	Symbol for work, head for human being and arrow showing out
	constructive dismissal	Symbol for dismissal with a wavy line for constructive
	unfair dismissal	Symbol for dismissal and symbol for negative (downturned mouth)
MHRT	Mental Health Review Tribunal	An initialism
S!	special	S with exclamation mark
	Transport Tribunal	Symbol for tribunal and symbol for transport
	chair	Symbol for chair (with head if it is a human being)

Tribunals (3)

SYMBOL	ENGLISH	EXPLANATION
	appeal hearing	Symbol for appeal and symbol for hearing
mgt	case management	Symbol for case and abbreviation for management
	employer	Symbol for work and head on top to indicate employer
	employee	Symbol for work and head inside to indicate employee
	notice	Symbol for dismissal and speech marks indicating that person states they are leaving
	be given notice	Symbol for notice with the hand added to indicate given
	job	Symbol for work with wavy line to weaken it into job
	dismissal of a case	Symbol for case and arrow to indicate dismissal

Tribunals (4)

SYMBOL	ENGLISH	EXPLANATION
	mental health	Symbol for head and symbol for health
	sick leave	Symbol for sick person and symbol for legs to indicate leave
	unpaid	Symbol for pay(ment) crossed out
	leave	Symbol for leave
Y	annual leave	Y for annual/yearly and symbol for leave
	maternity leave	Stick person with tummy to indicate pregnant and symbol for leave
	recorder	Symbol for tape and symbol for legal professional

Civil Law (1)

SYMBOL	ENGLISH	EXPLANATION
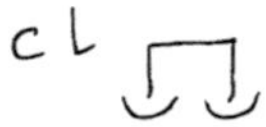	civil law	First and last letter of word and symbol for law
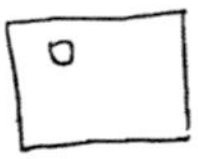	order	Symbol for sheet of paper and first letter of word
	applicant	Symbol of hand asking for something, first letter of word and head for human being
	bankruptcy	Symbol for money crossed out twice
	bankruptcy order	Symbol for bankruptcy and symbol for order
	liquidation	Symbol for money and wavy line to show liquid
	civil wrong	Symbol for civil and downturned mouth for wrong
	breach of contract	Symbol for sheet of paper with first letter of contract and symbol for breach

Civil Law (2)

SYMBOL	ENGLISH	EXPLANATION
c	contract law	Symbol for contract and symbol for law
t + c^{s}	terms and conditions	First letters of words and plural s
co	company law	Abbreviation for company and symbol for law
Co H	Companies House	First letters of words and roof for building
CAB	Citizens Advice Bureau	An initialism
HMRC	HM Revenue & Customs	An initialism
	infringement	Circle with two wavy lines going into it to show infringement

Civil Law (3)

SYMBOL	ENGLISH	EXPLANATION
	credit	Symbol for money and + for positive
	debit	Symbol for money and – for negative
	creditor	Symbol for credit and head for human being
	debtor	Symbol for debit and head for human being
	debt	Symbol for money underlined twice
	remedy (both legal & medical)	First letter of word capitalized with line to make circle look like a tablet (med.) i.e. a remedy
	statutory declaration	Symbol for sheet of paper, symbol for law and speech marks
	negligence	Symbol of hand with wavy line to show that it was negligent

Civil Law (4)

SYMBOL	ENGLISH	EXPLANATION
	truth	First letter of word made to look like a tick to show truth
	statement of truth	Symbol for statement and symbol for truth
	winding-up order	Symbol for order and X to show end
	will	Symbol for sheet of paper, symbol for dead person and speech marks
	testator	Symbol for dead person and speech marks
	intestate	Symbol for will with X for end (to show died without will)
	inheritance	Symbol for will and symbol for money
	inheritance law	Symbol for inheritance and symbol for law

Social Services (1)

SYMBOL	ENGLISH	EXPLANATION
SocS	Social Services	First three letters of first word and first letter of second word
	child neglect	Symbol for child and symbol for neglect
	child protection	Symbol for child and symbol for protection
	family liaison	Symbol for family and speech marks for liaison
	case worker	Symbol of sheet for case and symbol for worker
Soc	social worker	Symbol for social and symbol for worker
	foster home	Symbol of two people with last person in shape of F for fostering and roof for home
	care	Symbol for person on boat being looked after

Social Services (2)

SYMBOL	ENGLISH	EXPLANATION
→ ↥	take into care	Arrow to show take and symbol for care
	abuse	Person with wavy line into their head to indicate abuse
	adult abuse	Symbol for abuse and symbol for adult
	child abuse	Symbol for abuse and symbol for child
£ ∪	benefits	Symbol for money and smiling mouth
£ ∪	incapacity benefit	Person in wheelchair to indicate incapacity and symbol for benefit
FTC	family tax credit	First letter of each of the three words
	vulnerable adult	Symbol for adult with body in shape of wavy line to show weak

Social Services (3)

SYMBOL	ENGLISH	EXPLANATION
	day care	Symbol for care and d for day
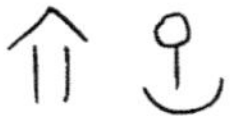	home care	Symbol for care and symbol for home
	care home	Symbol for care and roof to indicate home
	mental health issues	Abbreviation for mental health and symbol for problem
	emotional instability	Heart to indicate emotion and wavy line to indicate instability
	danger	Symbol for danger
	risk, at risk	Symbol for danger reduced to show risk
	at risk of abuse	Symbol for risk and symbol for abuse

Social Services (4)

SYMBOL	ENGLISH	EXPLANATION
	adoption	Symbol of two people with last person in shape of A for adoption
	leaving care	Symbol for care and arrow pointing outwards for leaving
	plan	Symbol invented by one of the authors which can be expanded
	project	Project is more than plan so an extra leg is added
	programme	Programme is more than a project and therefore another leg is added
SSI	Social Service Inspectorate	First letters of each word
DoH	Department of Health	Frequently used abbreviation

Housing (1)

SYMBOL	ENGLISH	EXPLANATION
	housing	Symbol for house and half circle to show overall concept
	housing office	Symbol for housing and second roof for office
	flat	Symbol for house with small cross to indicate a flat not a full house
 £	rented accommodation	Symbol for house and money to indicate it is rented
	semi-detached	Symbol for house and line to split it in half
	house	Symbol for house
	homeless / living on the streets	Symbol for house crossed out
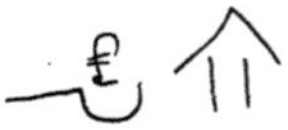 £	housing benefit	Symbol for benefit and symbol for house

Housing (2)

SYMBOL	ENGLISH	EXPLANATION
	move house	Symbol of two houses with arrow pointing from one to the other
CT_x	Council Tax	First letter of first word and Tx for tax
ins	insurance	First three letters of word
ins	building insurance	Symbol for building and symbol for insurance
ins	contents insurance	Symbol for insurance inside a house to show content
	building work	Symbol for building and symbol for work
	decorating	Decorating brush
	interior design	Symbol for decorating and roof to show inside a building

Housing (3)

SYMBOL	ENGLISH	EXPLANATION
	landlord	Symbol for house with hand giving housing
	tenant	Symbol for house and hand taking housing
	furnished	Chair with roof over it
	unfurnished	Symbol for furnished crossed out
	fully furnished	Symbol for furnished underlined
	sheltered accommodation	Symbol for house combined with symbol for protection
HO	housing officer	First two letters of words and head for human being
ch	central heating	Using abbreviation used by estate agents

Housing (4)

SYMBOL	ENGLISH	EXPLANATION
ff.	fridge freezer	Using abbreviation used by estate agents
°C –	cold	Symbol for degrees centigrade and – to show cold
°C +	warm	Symbol for degrees centigrade and + to show warm
°C –	wind chill factor	Symbol for cold and three lines for wind blowing
£>	bills	Symbol for sheet of paper and symbol for outgoings
£>	water bill	Symbol for bill and symbol for water
	lodger	Symbol for house and symbol for human being with wavy line as body to indicate they are not the owner

Health (1)

SYMBOL	ENGLISH	EXPLANATION
	health	Symbol often used by chemists - a snake wrapped around a stick
	body	Stick man with thick body
	doctor	Symbol for health with head for human being
	nurse	Symbol for doctor with wavy line to differentiate between doctor and nurse
	hospital	Symbol for health and roof for building
GP	General Practitioner	Commonly used abbreviation
GP	GP's surgery	Symbol for GP with roof for building
	medicine	A tablet

Health (2)

SYMBOL	ENGLISH	EXPLANATION
	ill	Someone lying down/in bed as they are ill
	illness	First letter of word with long line (to be expanded upon later)
	dead	Symbol for dead
	healthy	Symbol for ill crossed out to show opposite
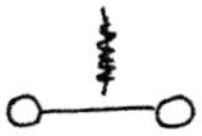	ambulance	Symbol for vehicle and symbol for health
	home visit	Symbol for home and symbol for visit
	health care centre	Symbol for health, symbol for care and roof to indicate centre
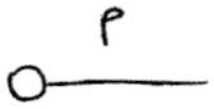 P	patient	Symbol for ill and P for patient

Health (3)

SYMBOL	ENGLISH	EXPLANATION
	patient confidentiality	Symbol for patient and square brackets to indicate confidentiality
	wound	Symbol for ill with dent showing injury/wound
	stretcher	Simplified drawing of a stretcher
	diabetes	Symbol for illness and first letter of word diabetes
	coronary heart disease	Symbol for illness and first letters of three words
	consultation	Symbol for doctor and speech marks for consultation
	bones	Simplified drawing of rib cage
	surgery	Symbol of ill person with two knives used for surgery

Health (4)

SYMBOL	ENGLISH	EXPLANATION
	pressure	Surface with arrow pointing onto it to indicate pressure
 B	blood	Symbol for liquid and b for blood
 B	blood pressure	Symbol for blood and symbol for pressure
 F	flu	Symbol for illness and first letter of word flu
	fracture	Symbol for ill person with zigzag line to indicate a break
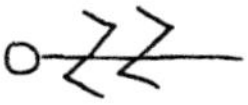	open fracture	Symbol for ill person with two zigzag lines to indicate an open fracture
	vomiting	Head with two lines out of mouth to indicate being sick
	nose bleed	Symbol for nose with blood drops coming out of it

Mental Health (1)

SYMBOL	ENGLISH	EXPLANATION
[illegible]	mental health	Symbol for mental health
PSY	psychosis	Symbol for illness and first three letters of word psychosis
[illegible]	depression	Symbol for illness and face with a downturned mouth to show sadness
MHS	Mental Health Services	An initialism
Th	therapy	Capital T and lower case h
"Th	talking therapies	Symbol for therapy and speech marks to indicate talking
[illegible]	schizophrenia	Symbol for illness and two people joined up to indicate dual personality
[illegible]	paranoid schizophrenia	Symbol for schizophrenia and head with eyes watching to indicate paranoia

Mental Health (2)

SYMBOL	ENGLISH	EXPLANATION
PS "	psychology	First two letters of word and speech marks (to differentiate from psychiatry)
PS ⊘	psychiatry	First two letters of word and tablet (to differentiate from psychology)
W over □	ward	Square for room and W to indicate a ward
W over □ with arrow	to admit to a ward	Symbol for ward and arrow pointing in to show admission
W over □ with door	closed ward	Symbol for ward with door opening to inside to indicate closed
W over □ with door	open ward	Symbol for ward with door opening outwards to indicate open
MHA	Mental Health Act	An initialism

Mental Health (3)

SYMBOL	ENGLISH	EXPLANATION
	terror, panic	Face with eyes wide open and hair standing on end
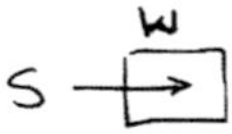	sectioning	Symbol for ward and s with arrow into ward
	medication	Tablet
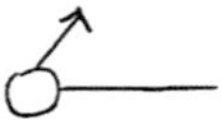	self harm	Symbol for ill/injured person with arrow pointing out of person
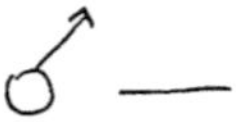	suicide	Symbol for dead person with arrow pointing out of person
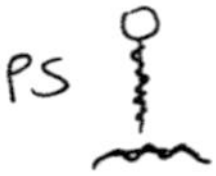	psychiatric nurse	Symbol for psychiatry and symbol for nurse
	delusions	Head with coil coming out of it
	delusions of grandeur	Symbol for delusions underlined for emphasis

Mental Health (4)

SYMBOL	ENGLISH	EXPLANATION
Prz	Prozac	Abbreviation
	anti-depressant	Symbol for tablet over the symbol for depression
	hyper active	Symbol of head with flailing arms
	hyper active child	Symbol for hyperactive and symbol for child
bp	bipolar disorder	Symbol for illness and first letters of words
	protection	Umbrella for protection
soc	approved social worker	Symbol for social, symbol for worker and tick for approved

CHAPTER 8

SOURCES OF SYMBOLS

Musical Notes

Musical notes and symbols are very useful (not only to those who already play an instrument and know how to read them) as they have specific values and meanings already attached to them.

This is only a very short extract to give you an idea of which symbols could be used to, e.g. add or 'erase' certain values to already existing symbols.

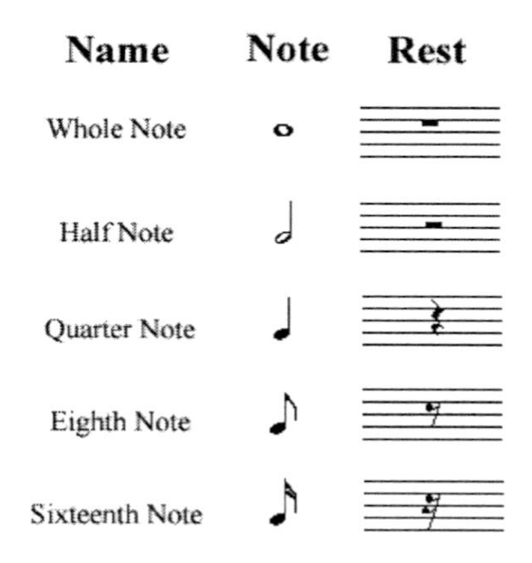

Name
Note
Rest
Whole Note
Half Note
Quarter Note
Eighth Note
Sixteenth Note

'erases' the value given to the note

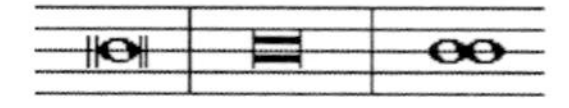

Some UK Traffic Signs

Traffic signs from all countries are very useful as they are in themselves already very precise, translate a certain concept visually, are easily understood and are already well known to drivers. As they have a very basic underlying structure, they can easily be adapted for use as a symbol.

[red triangle only]

Other danger; plate indicates nature of danger

Road works

Falling or fallen rocks

[red circle only, same as no vehicles]

No vehicles

No pedestrians

No cycling

No vehicles with over 12 seats except regular scheduled, school and work buses

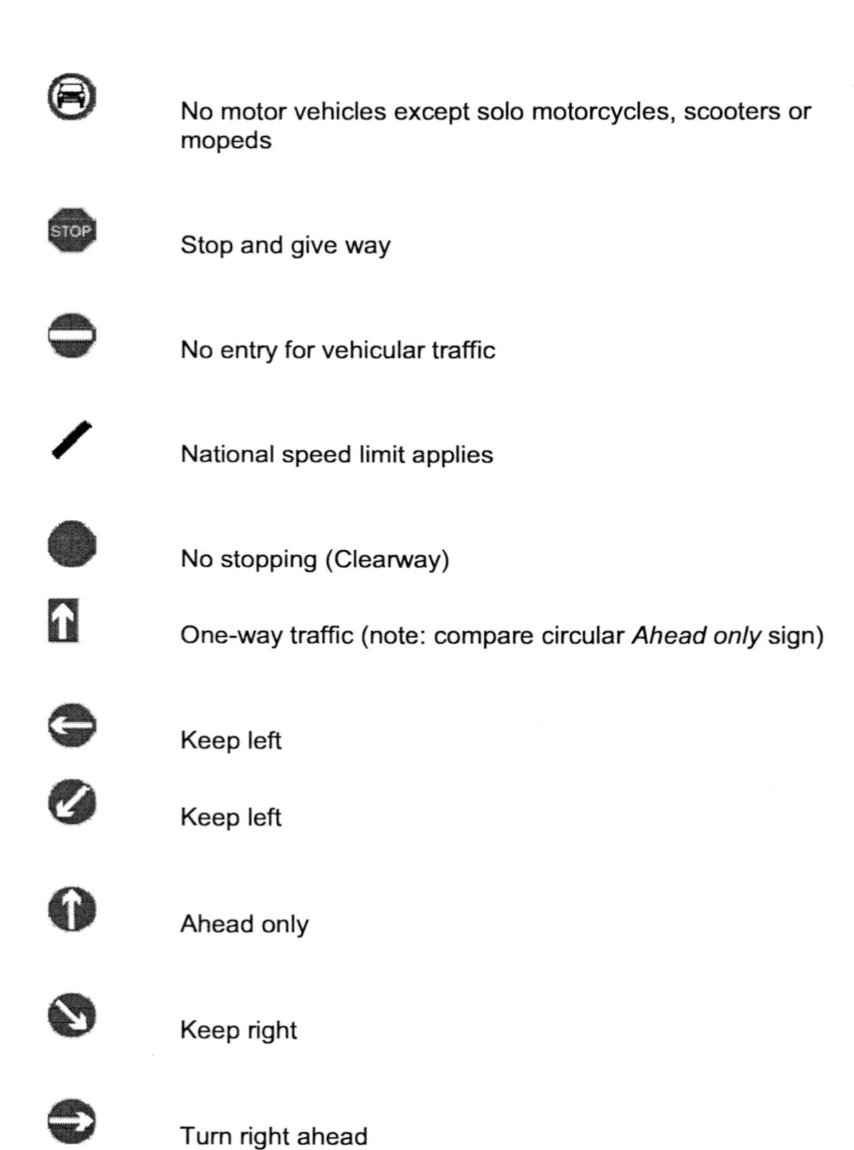

No motor vehicles except solo motorcycles, scooters or mopeds

Stop and give way

No entry for vehicular traffic

National speed limit applies

No stopping (Clearway)

One-way traffic (note: compare circular *Ahead only* sign)

Keep left

Keep left

Ahead only

Keep right

Turn right ahead

Olympic Pictograms (1972 Olympic Games in Munich)

These pictograms were used at the 1972 Olympic Games in Munich, Germany in order to limit the verbal information used at such a massive multi-lingual event. Even without the explanations given, you are able to understand these pictures. This is the symbol of "stick man" used earlier in the book in an expanded version.

Some Emoticons

Even internet and mobile phone chat novices amongst us are aware of some of the simple and most commonly used emoticons like a happy or sad smiley. Emoticons such as those used on Yahoo or MSN Messenger are a valuable source of symbols for emotions as the more complex emotions like anger or tiredness are difficult to capture in an easily recognizable symbol.

Below you will find a short list of emotions, the original emoticon depicting them. The keyboard key should be used as symbol in note-taking as it portrays the smileys' facial expression.

Original emoticon	Keyboard keys for symbol use	Original meaning	Further meanings
	:)	happy	content, pleased, joyful, cheerful, glad, blissful
	:(	sad	unhappy, miserable, down, depressing, gloomy
	:-/	confused	baffled, puzzled, perplexed, bewildered, mystified
	:">	blushing	shy, coy, timid, reserved, retiring, withdrawn
	=((	broken hearted	crestfallen, disappointed, deflated
	:-O	surprise	shock, revelation, disclosure, astonishment

	X(	angry	annoyed, irritated, fuming, irate, livid, heated
	:>	smug	self-satisfied, superior, self-righteous, arrogant
	:-S	worried	concerned, anxious, apprehensive, nervous, troubled
	:((	crying	lament, weeping, expression of grief, sobbing
	:))	laughing	smiling, amused, pleased, chuckling, giggling
	:|	straight face	earnest, serious, solemn, sober, formal, grave, sincere
	:-<	sigh	moan, groan, relieved, calmed, reassured, thankful

Periodic table

The periodic table provides you with a short abbreviation for otherwise difficult chemical elements. As most elements, apart from widely used metals such as iron, gold or silver, are rarely used it is advisable to learn these on a needs basis and then use them together with your symbol for *metal* (e.g. M/).

Name chemical element	**Symbol**
Actinium	**Ac**
Aluminum	**Al**
Americium	**Am**
Antimony	**Sb**
Argon	**Ar**
Arsenic	**As**
Astatine	**At**
Barium	**Ba**
Berkelium	**Bk**
Beryllium	**Be**
Bismuth	**Bi**
Bohrium	**Bh**
Boron	**B**
Bromine	**Br**
Cadmium	**Cd**
Calcium	**Ca**
Californium	**Cf**
Carbon	**C**
Cerium	**Ce**

Name chemical element	**Symbol**
Cesium	**Cs**
Chlorine	**Cl**
Chromium	**Cr**
Cobalt	**Co**
Copper	**Cu**
Curium	**Cm**
Darmstadtium	**Ds**
Dubnium	**Db**
Dysprosium	**Dy**
Einsteinium	**Es**
Erbium	**Er**
Europium	**Eu**
Fermium	**Fm**
Fluorine	**F**
Francium	**Fr**
Gadolinium	**Gd**
Gallium	**Ga**
Germanium	**Ge**
Gold	**Au**

Hafnium	Hf
Hassium	Hs
Helium	He
Holmium	Ho
Hydrogen	H
Indium	In
Iodine	I
Iridium	Ir
Iron	Fe
Krypton	Kr
Lanthanum	La
Lawrencium	Lr
Lead	Pb
Lithium	Li
Lutetium	Lu
Magnesium	Mg
Manganese	Mn
Meitnerium	Mt
Mendelevium	Md
Mercury	Hg
Molybdenum	Mo
Neodymium	Nd
Neon	Ne
Neptunium	Np
Nickel	Ni
Niobium	Nb

Nitrogen	N
Nobelium	No
Osmium	Os
Oxygen	O
Palladium	Pd
Phosphorus	P
Platinum	Pt
Plutonium	Pu
Polonium	Po
Potassium	K
Praseodymium	Pr
Promethium	Pm
Protactinium	Pa
Radium	Ra
Radon	Rn
Rhenium	Re
Rhodium	Rh
Rubidium	Rb
Ruthenium	Ru
Rutherfordium	Rf
Samarium	Sm
Scandium	Sc
Seaborgium	Sg
Selenium	Se
Silicon	Si
Silver	Ag

Sodium	Na
Strontium	Sr
Sulfur	S
Tantalum	Ta
Technetium	Tc
Tellurium	Te
Terbium	Tb
Thallium	Tl
Thorium	Th
Thulium	Tm
Tin	Sn
Titanium	Ti
Tungsten	W
Ununbium	Uub
Ununhexium	Uuh
Ununoctium	Uuo
Ununpentium	Uup
Ununquadium	Uuq
Ununseptium	Uus
Ununtrium	Uut
Ununium	Uuu
Uranium	U
Vanadium	V
Xenon	Xe
Ytterbium	Yb
Yttrium	Y

Zinc	Zn
Zirconium	Zr

A Selection of Alphabets

Although we can all read and write and have learned to make use of at least one alphabet enabling us to do so, knowledge of one, two or even three alphabets is still very limiting with regard to note-taking.

It proves very useful to use foreign and ancient languages' alphabets, writing systems and symbols - not learning to read them necessarily, but extracting all those symbols that can be easily written and remembered.

As most of these symbols, letters and logograms have been developed over centuries, most of them are very concise and convey (in the case of simple logograms) specific information. Such symbols should be used to convey the value (meaning) they have already been given, although slight modifications might be necessary. Abstract symbols can be allocated a meaning of your own choice.

Many of the symbols may not seem useful at first, but a glossary of these symbols can be used for inspiration when you are struggling to develop new symbols.

On the following pages you will find a selection of some foreign and ancient languages' alphabets, writing systems and symbols. Please be aware that this is merely an excerpt and is by no means a complete list.

Phonetic alphabet

THE INTERNATIONAL PHONETIC ALPHABET (2005)

CONSONANTS (PULMONIC)

	Bilabial	Labio-dental	Dental	Alveolar	Post-alveolar	Retroflex	Palatal	Velar	Uvular	Pharyngeal	Epi-glottal	Glottal
Nasal	m	ɱ		n		ɳ	ɲ	ŋ	ɴ			
Plosive	p b	ȹ ȸ		t d		ʈ ɖ	c ɟ	k ɡ	q ɢ		ʡ	ʔ
Fricative	ɸ β	f v	θ ð	s z	ʃ ʒ	ʂ ʐ	ç ʝ	x ɣ	χ ʁ	ħ ʕ	ʜ ʢ	h ɦ
Approximant		ʋ		ɹ		ɻ	j	ɰ				
Trill	ʙ			r					ʀ		я	
Tap, Flap		ⱱ		ɾ		ɽ						
Lateral fricative				ɬ ɮ		ꞎ	𝼆	𝼄				
Lateral approximant				l		ɭ	ʎ	ʟ				
Lateral flap				ɺ		𝼈						

Where symbols appear in pairs, the one to the right represents a modally voiced consonant, except for murmured ɦ.
Shaded areas denote articulations judged to be impossible. Light grey letters are unofficial extensions of the IPA.

CONSONANTS (NON-PULMONIC)

Anterior click releases (require posterior stops)	Voiced implosives	Ejectives
ʘ Bilabial fricated	ɓ Bilabial	ʼ *Examples:*
ǀ Laminal alveolar fricated ("dental")	ɗ Dental or alveolar	pʼ Bilabial
ǃ Apical (post)alveolar abrupt ("retroflex")	ʄ Palatal	tʼ Dental or alveolar
ǂ Laminal postalveolar abrupt ("palatal")	ɠ Velar	kʼ Velar
ǁ Lateral alveolar fricated ("lateral")	ʛ Uvular	sʼ Alveolar fricative

CONSONANTS (CO-ARTICULATED)

ʍ Voiceless labialized velar approximant
w Voiced labialized velar approximant
ɥ Voiced labialized palatal approximant
ɕ Voiceless palatalized postalveolar (alveolo-palatal) fricative
ʑ Voiced palatalized postalveolar (alveolo-palatal) fricative
ɧ Simultaneous x and ʃ (disputed)
k͡p t͡s Affricates and double articulations may be joined by a tie bar

VOWELS

	Front	Near front	Central	Near back	Back
Close	i • y		ɨ • ʉ		ɯ • u
Near close		ɪ • ʏ		• ʊ	
Close mid	e • ø		ɘ • ɵ		ɤ • o
Mid			ə		
Open mid	ɛ • œ		ɜ • ɞ		ʌ • ɔ
Near open	æ		ɐ		
Open	a • ɶ				ɑ • ɒ

Vowels at right & left of bullets are rounded & unrounded.

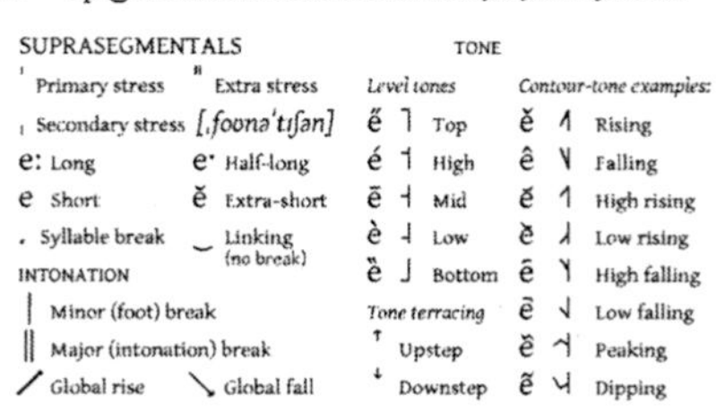

SUPRASEGMENTALS
ˈ Primary stress
ˈˈ Extra stress
ˌ Secondary stress [ˌfoʊnəˈtɪʃən]
eː Long
eˑ Half-long
e Short
ĕ Extra-short
. Syllable break
‿ Linking (no break)
INTONATION
| Minor (foot) break
‖ Major (intonation) break
↗ Global rise
↘ Global fall
TONE
Level tones
e̋ ˥ Top
é ˦ High
ē ˧ Mid
è ˨ Low
ȅ ˩ Bottom
Tone terracing
ꜛ Upstep
ꜜ Downstep
Contour-tone examples:
ě ˩˥ Rising
ê ˥˩ Falling
e᷄ ˧˥ High rising
e᷅ ˩˧ Low rising
e᷇ ˥˧ High falling
e᷆ ˧˩ Low falling
e᷈ ˧˦˧ Peaking
e᷉ ˧˨˧ Dipping

DIACRITICS

Diacritics may be placed above a symbol with a descender, as ŋ̊. Other IPA symbols may appear as diacritics to represent phonetic detail: tˢ (fricative release), bʱ (breathy voice), ˀa (glottal onset), ᵊ (epenthetic schwa), oᶷ (diphthongization).

SYLLABICITY & RELEASES		PHONATION		PRIMARY ARTICULATION		SECONDARY ARTICULATION			
n̩ ɹ̩	Syllabic	n̥ d̥	Voiceless or Slack voice	t̪ b̪	Dental	tʷ dʷ	Labialized	ɔ̹ x̹	More rounded
e̯ ʊ̯	Non-syllabic	s̬ d̬	Modal voice or Stiff voice	t̺ d̺	Apical	tʲ dʲ	Palatalized	ɔ̜ xʷ̜	Less rounded
tʰ ʰt	(Pre)aspirated	n̤ a̤	Breathy voice	t̻ d̻	Laminal	tˠ dˠ	Velarized	ẽ z̃	Nasalized
dⁿ	Nasal release	n̰ a̰	Creaky voice	u̟ t̟	Advanced	tˤ dˤ	Pharyngealized	ɚ ɝ	Rhoticity
dˡ	Lateral release	n̪͆ a̪͆	Strident	i̠ t̠	Retracted	ɫ z̴	Velarized or pharyngealized	e̘ o̘	Advanced tongue root
t̚	No audible release	n̼ d̼	Linguolabial	ä ÿ	Centralized	ɯ̽	Mid-centralized	e̙ o̙	Retracted tongue root
e̞ β̞	Lowered (β̞ is a bilabial approximant)			e̝ ɹ̝	Raised (ɹ̝ is a voiced alveolar non-sibilant fricative)				

Arkadian

	Ca	Ce	Ci	Cu	aC	eC	iC	uC
	𒀀	𒂊	𒄿	𒌋				
k	𒅗	𒆠		𒆪				
g	𒂵	𒄀		𒄖	𒀝		𒅅	𒌊
q	𒋡	𒆥		𒄣				
p	𒉺	𒉿		𒁍	𒀊	𒅁		𒌒
b	𒁀	𒁉						
t	𒋫	𒋼	𒋾	𒌅	𒀜	𒀉		𒌓
d	𒁕		𒁲	𒁺				
m	𒈠	𒈨	𒈪	𒈬	𒄠		𒅎	𒌝
n	𒈾	𒉈	𒉌	𒉡	𒀭	𒂗	𒅔	𒌦
s	𒊓	𒋛		𒋢				
z	𒍝	𒍣		𒍪	𒊍		𒄑	
ṣ	𒍝	𒍢		𒍮				
š	𒊭	𒊺	𒅆	𒋗	𒀸	𒌍	𒅖	𒍑
h	𒄩	𒄭		𒄷	𒄴			𒌔
l	𒆷	𒇷		𒇻	𒀠	𒂖	𒅋	𒌌
r	𒊏	𒊑		𒊒	𒅈		𒅕	𒌨
y	𒅀							
'	𒀪							

Arabic Naskhi script

Name	Phonetic	Isolated	Final	Medial	Initial
alif	[ʔ]	ا	ـا		
ba:	[b]	ب	ـب	ـبـ	بـ
ta:	[t]	ت	ـت	ـتـ	تـ
tha:	[θ]	ث	ـث	ـثـ	ثـ
ji:m	[j]	ج	ـج	ـجـ	جـ
ḥa:	[ħ]	ح	ـح	ـحـ	حـ
kha:	[x]	خ	ـخ	ـخـ	خـ
da:l	[d]	د	ـد		
dha:l	[ð]	ذ	ـذ		
ra:	[r]	ر	ـر		
za:	[z]	ز	ـز		
si:n	[s]	س	ـس	ـسـ	سـ
shi:n	[š]	ش	ـش	ـشـ	شـ
sa:d	[s]	ص	ـص	ـصـ	صـ
ḍa:d	[ḍ]	ض	ـض	ـضـ	ضـ
ṭa:	[ṭ]	ط	ـط	ـطـ	طـ
ẓa:	[ẓ]	ظ	ـظ	ـظـ	ظـ
'ain	[ʕ]	ع	ـع	ـعـ	عـ
ghain	[ʁ]	غ	ـغ	ـغـ	غـ
fa:	[f]	ف	ـف	ـفـ	فـ
qa:f	[q]	ق	ـق	ـقـ	قـ
ka:f	[k]	ك	ـك	ـكـ	كـ
la:m	[l]	ل	ـل	ـلـ	لـ
mi:m	[m]	م	ـم	ـمـ	مـ
nu:n	[n]	ن	ـن	ـنـ	نـ
ha:	[h]	ه	ـه	ـهـ	هـ
wa:w	[w]	و	ـو		
ya:	[y]	ي	ـي	ـيـ	يـ

Armenian

letter	name	EA	WA	letter	name	EA	WA
Ա ա	aib	a	a	Մ մ	mem	m	m
Բ բ	ben	b	p^h	Յ յ	hi	y	y
Գ գ	gim	g	k^h	Ն ն	nu	n	n
Դ դ	da	d	t^h	Շ շ	ša	š	š
Ե ե	yeč^h	e, ye-	e, ye-	Ո ո	vo	o, vo-	o, vo-
Զ զ	za	z	z	Չ չ	č^{h}a	č^h	č^h
Է է	e	e	e	Պ պ	pe	p	b
Ը ը	ət^h	ə	ə	Ջ ջ	ǰe	ǰ	č^h
Թ թ	t^ho	t^h	t^h	Ռ ռ	rra	rr	rr
Ժ ժ	že	ž	ž	Ս ս	se	s	s
Ի ի	ini	i	i	Վ վ	vev	v	v
Լ լ	lyun	l	l	Տ տ	tyun	t	d
Խ խ	xe	x	x	Ր ր	re	r	r
Ծ ծ	tsa	ts	dz	Ց ց	ts^{h}o	ts^h	ts^h
Կ կ	ken	k	g	Ւ ւ	hyun	v, u	v, u
Հ հ	ho	h	h	Փ փ	p^hyur	p^h	p^h
Ձ ձ	dza	dz	ts	Ք ք	k^he	k^h	k^h
Ղ ղ	yad	y	y	Օ օ	o	o	o
Ճ ճ	če	č	ǰ	Ֆ ֆ	fe	f	f

Avestan

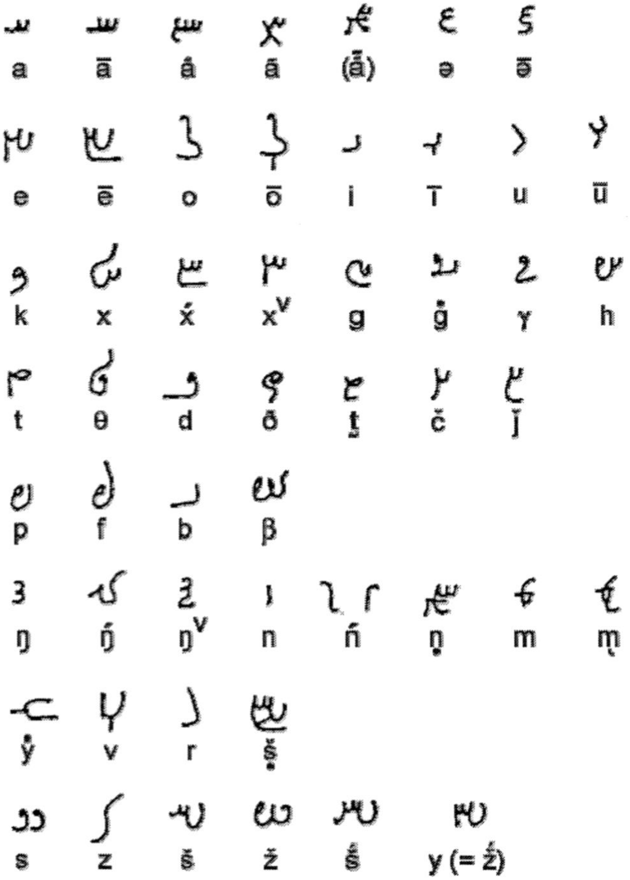

a	ā	å	ą	(ą̊)	ə	ə̄	
e	ē	o	ō	i	ī	u	ū
k	x	x́	x^v	g	ġ	γ	h
t	θ	d	δ	t̰	č	ǰ	
p	f	b	β				
ŋ	ŋ́	$ŋ^v$	n	ń	ṇ	m	m̨
ẏ	v	r	š̩				
s	z	š	ž	ṣ̌	y (= ž́)		

Berber & Tifinagh

	ANCIENT BERBER		TIFINIGH	
	horizontal	vertical	letter	ligature w/ t
ʼ	·	·	·	
b	⊙	⊙ ⊡	⦶ ◫	+◫
ğ	Γ	V Λ	·|· ÷	‡
d	Π	⊐ ⊏	Π Λ	
h		||||	⋮	
w	=	‖	:	
z	—	—	#	#
ž	H	H I	I	
ẓ	⋔	Ш	ⵣ ⵥ	
ḫ	⊢	⊥ ⊤	∷	
ṭ, ḍ	≻—	ᗰ	Ǝ E Ш	
y	Z	N Z	{ }	
k	⇐	⇈	·:	
l	‖	=	‖	⊢|

g				
r				
š				
t				
t^2				

Brahmi

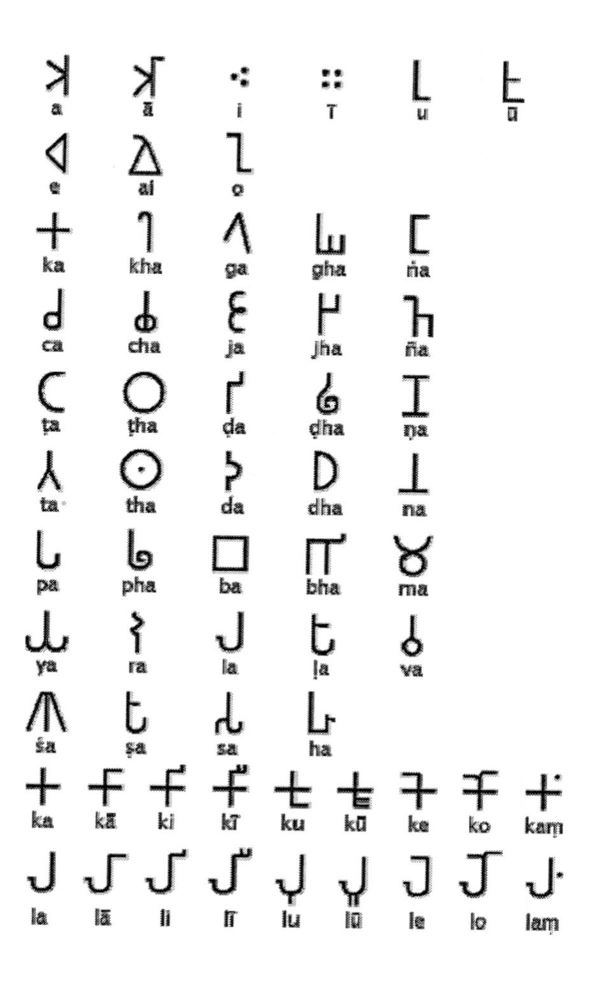
a ā i ī u ū
e ai o
ka kha ga gha ṅa
ca cha ja jha ña
ṭa ṭha ḍa ḍha ṇa
ta tha da dha na
pa pha ba bha ma
ya ra la ḷa va
śa ṣa sa ha
ka kā ki kī ku kū ke ko kaṃ
la lā li lī lu lū le lo laṃ

Bugis

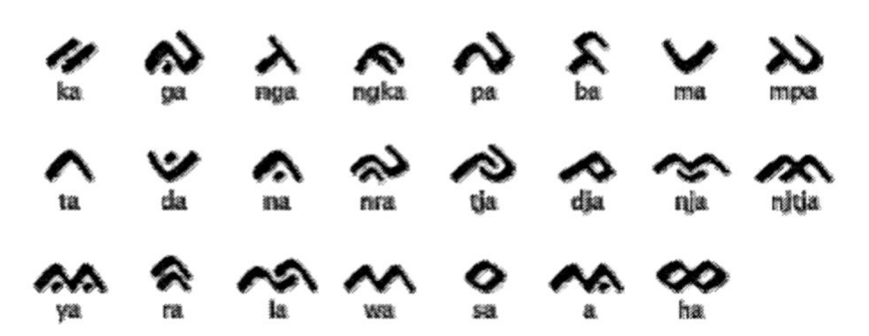
ka ga nga ngka pa ba ma mpa
ta da na nra tja dja nja njtja
ya ra la wa sa a ha

Burmese

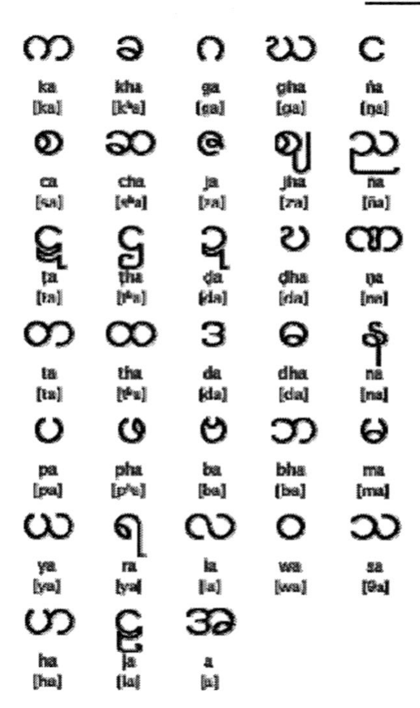
ka kha ga gha ṅa
ca cha ja jha ña
ṭa ṭha ḍa ḍha ṇa
ta tha da dha na
pa pha ba bha ma
ya ra la wa sa
ha ḷa a

creaky	မ	မိ	မု	မေ့	မဲ့	မို့	မော့
	a [á]	i [í]	u [ú]	ẹ [é]	aị [ɛ́]	uị [ó]	ọ [ɔ́]
low	မာ	မီ	မူ	မေ	မယ်	မို	မော်
	ā [a]	ī [i]	ū [u]	e [e]	ay [ɛ]	ui [o]	ō [ɔ]
high	မား	မီး	မူး	မေး	မဲ	မိုး	မော
	a: [à]	i: [ì]	u: [ù]	e: [è]	ai [ɛ̀]	ui: [ò]	o [ɔ̀]

ဣ	ဤ	ဥ	ဦ	ဦး	ဧ	ဩ	ဪ
í	i	ú	u	ù	e	ɔ	ɔ̀

ဆင်	သိပ်	ဩဂုတ်
can	sip	ogut

ကြ	ကွ	ကျ	မှ
kra	kwa	kya	mha

၀	၁	၂	၃	၄	၅	၆	၇	၈	၉
0	1	2	3	4	5	6	7	8	9

Cypriot

a	e	i	o	u
ja			jo	
ka	ke	ki	ko	ku
la	le	li	lo	lu
ma	me	mi	mo	mu
na	ne	ni	no	nu
pa	pe	pi	po	pu
ra	re	ri	ro	ru
sa	se	si	so	su
ta	te	ti	to	tu
wa	we	wi	wo	
xa	xe		zo	
ga				

Devanagari

अ	आ	इ	ई	उ	ऊ
a	ā	i	ī	u	ū
ऋ	ॠ	ऌ	ॡ		
ṛ	ṝ	ḷ	ḹ		
ए	ऐ	ओ	औ	अं	अः
e	ai	o	au	aṃ	aḥ
क	ख	ग	घ	ङ	
ka	kha	ga	gha	ṅa	
च	छ	ज	झ	ञ	
ca	cha	ja	jha	ña	
ट	ठ	ड	ढ	ण	
ṭa	ṭha	ḍa	ḍha	ṇa	
त	थ	द	ध	न	
ta	tha	da	dha	na	
प	फ	ब	भ	म	
pa	pha	ba	bha	ma	
य	र	ल	व		
ya	ra	la	va		
श	ष	स	ह		
śa	ṣa	sa	ha		

Egyptian

glyph	translit.	phonetic	glyph	translit.	phonetic
	ȝ	[ʔ]		*ḥ*	[ħ]
	i	[i]		*ḫ*	[x]
	y	[y]		*ẖ*	[ç]
	ʿ	[ʕ]		*s*	[s]
	w	[w]		*š*	[š]
	b	[b]		*ḳ*	[q]
	p	[p]		*k*	[k]
	f	[f]		*g*	[g]
	m	[m]		*t*	[t]
	n	[n]		*ṯ*	[tʸ], [c]
	r	[r]		*d*	[d]
	h	[h]		*ḏ*	[dʸ], [ɟ]

biconsonantal

	ir		*mr*		*sw*
	wp		*ms*		*kȝ*
	wr		*nb*		*sȝ*
	mn		*rw*		*ḏd*

triconsonantal

	ʿnḫ		*rwḏ*
	wȝḥ		*ḥtp*
	nfr		*ḫpr*
	nṯr		*šmʿ*

Etruscan

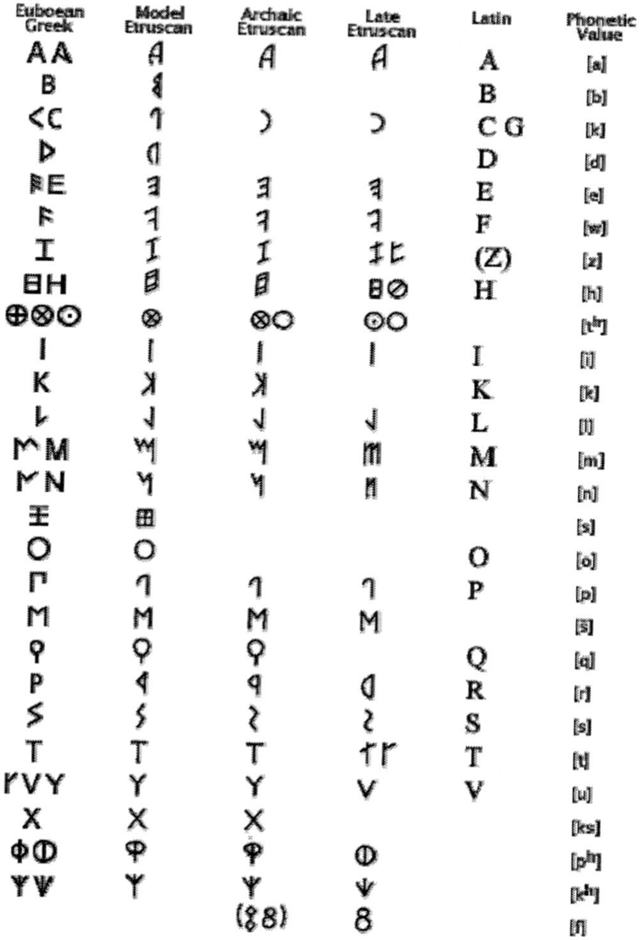

Euboean Greek	Model Etruscan	Archaic Etruscan	Late Etruscan	Latin	Phonetic Value
Α Α	𐌀	𐌀	𐌀	A	[a]
Β	𐌁			B	[b]
< C	𐌂	𐌂	𐌂	C G	[k]
Δ	𐌃			D	[d]
𐌄 E	𐌄	𐌄	𐌄	E	[e]
Ϝ	𐌅	𐌅	𐌅	F	[w]
I	𐌆	𐌆	𐌆	(Z)	[z]
⊟ H	𐌇	𐌇	𐌇 ⊘	H	[h]
⊕ ⊗ ⊙	⊗	⊗ O	⊙ O		$[t^h]$
I	I	I	I	I	[i]
K	𐌊	𐌊		K	[k]
𐌋	𐌋	𐌋	𐌋	L	[l]
𐌌 M	𐌌	𐌌	𐌌	M	[m]
𐌍 N	𐌍	𐌍	𐌍	N	[n]
Ξ	⊞				[s]
O	O			O	[o]
Γ	𐌐	𐌐	𐌐	P	[p]
M	M	M	M		[š]
Ϙ	Ϙ	Ϙ		Q	[q]
P	𐌓	𐌓	𐌓	R	[r]
≶	𐌔	𐌔	𐌔	S	[s]
T	T	T	𐌕	T	[t]
Y V Y	Y	Y	V	V	[u]
X	X	X			[ks]
Φ Φ	Φ	Φ	Φ		$[p^h]$
Ψ Ψ	Ψ	Ψ	Ψ		$[k^h]$
		(𐌚 8)	8		[f]

Futhark

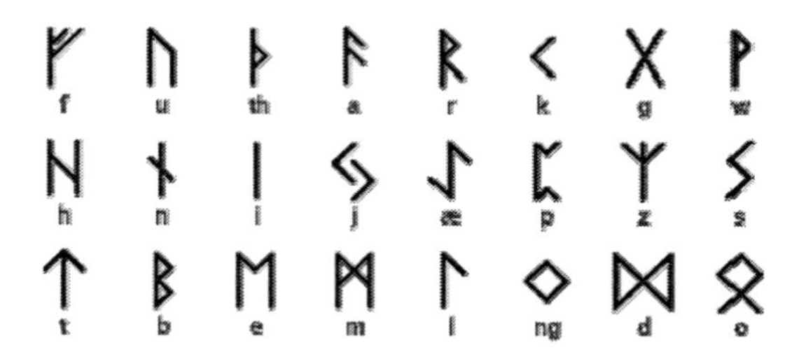

Galgolitic

a	b	v	g	d	ε	ž	dz
z	i	i	ǵ	k	l	m	n
ɔ	p	r	s	t	u	f	x (kh)
ɔ	ts	č	š	št	w/ə	ɨ	y
æ/e	yu	ɛ̃	yɛ̃	ɔ̃	yɔ̃	f	i/v

Linear B

Luwian

á à i í u ha há hi hu
ka ki ku la lá/lí li lì
ma mi mí mì mu na ná ni ní nu nú
pa pá pi pu ra/ri ru rú
sa sá sà sa4 sa5 sa6 sa7 si sí su sú sù
ta tá tà ta4 ta5 ti tí tu tú tù
wa/wi wá/wí wà/wì ia iá ià
za zá zà za4 zi zí zì zi4 zu

ANNUS 'year'
ARHA* 'away'
AUDIRE 'hear'
AVIS 'bird'
AVUS 'ancestor'
BONUS 'good'
BOS 'cow'
CAELUM 'heaven'
CAPUT 'head'
CASTRUM 'camp'
CERVUS 'stag'
CERVUS$_2$ 'stag'
CORNU 'horn'
CRUS 'leg'
CRUX 'cross'
CULTER 'knife'
CUM 'with'
CURRUS 'chariot'
DARE 'give'
DEUS 'god'
DOMINUS 'lord'
DOMUS 'house'
EGO 'I'
EQUUS 'horse'
EXERCITUS 'army'
FEMINA 'woman'
FINES 'boundary'
FRONS 'forehead'
HALPA* 'Aleppo'
HEROS 'hero'
INFANS 'child'
INFRA 'below'
IRA 'wrath'
LEPUS 'hare'
LIBARE 'offer'
LINGUA 'tongue'
LITUUS 'staff'
LOQUI 'speak'
LUNA 'moon'
MAGNUS 'great'
MALLEUS 'hammer'
MALUS 'bad'
MANUS 'hand'
MONS 'mountain'
NEG *negation*
NEG$_2$ *negation*
NEG$_3$ *negation*
NEPOS 'descendant'
OCCIDENS 'west'
OMNIS 'all'
ORIENS 'east'
OVIS 'sheep'
PANIS 'bread'
PES 'foot'
PES$_2$ 'foot'
PONERE 'put'
POST 'after'
PRAE 'before'
PUGNUS 'fist'
REGIO 'kingdom'
REX 'king'
SARMA* 'Sarruma'
SCALPRUM 'chisel'
SCRIBA 'clerk'
SOL 'sun'
SOLIUM 'seat'
STELE 'stela'
SUPER 'above'
TERRA 'land'
THRONUS 'throne'
TONITRUS 'thunder'
URBS 'city'
VAS 'vase'
VERSUS 'toward'
VIA 'road'
VINUM 'wine'
VIR 'man'
VIS 'strength'

Meroïtic

hiero.	cursive	value	hiero.	cursive	value	hiero.	cursive	value
		[a]			[m]			[se]
		[e]			[n]			[k]
		[i]			[ne]			[q]
		[o]			[r]			[t]
		[y]			[l]			[te]
		[w]			[ḫ]			[to]
		[b]			[ẖ]			[d]
		[p]			[š], [s]			*word divider*

Oscan

	a	[a]		h	[x]		r	[r]
	b	[b]		i	[i]		s	[s]
	g	[g]		k	[k]		t	[t]
	d	[d]		l	[l]		u	[u]
	e	[e]		m	[m]		f	[f]
	v	[v]		n	[n]		í	[iː]
	z	[dz]		p	[p]		ú	[uː]

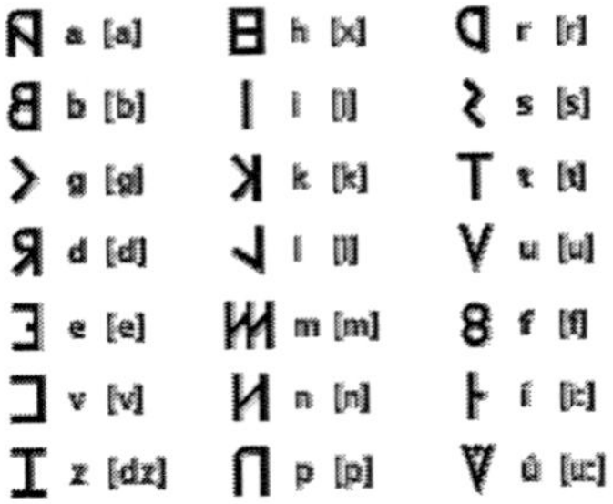

Phoenician

Letter	Name	Sound
𐤀	ʾaleph	[ʾ]
𐤁	beth	[b]
𐤂	gimmel	[g]
𐤃	daleth	[d]
𐤄	he	[h]
𐤅	waw	[w]
𐤆	zayin	[z]
𐤇	heth	[ḥ]
𐤈	teth	[ṭ]
𐤉	yodh	[y]
𐤊	kaph	[k]
𐤋	lamedh	[l]
𐤌	mem	[m]
𐤍	nun	[n]
𐤎	samekh	[s]
𐤏	ʿayin	[ʿ]
𐤐	pe	[p]
𐤑	tsade	[ṣ]
𐤒	qoph	[q]
𐤓	reš	[r]
𐤔	šin	[š]
𐤕	taw	[t]

Proto-Sinaitic

Letter Name	Proto-Sinaitic	Early Phoenician	Greek	Phonetic Value	Letter Meaning
ʾaleph			Α	[ʾ]	ox
beth			Β	[b]	house
gimmel			Γ	[g]	throwstick
daleth			Δ	[d]	door
he			Ε	[h]	
waw			Ϝ[1] Υ	[w]	hook/peg
zayin			Ζ	[z]	
heth			Η	[ḥ]	fence
teth			Θ	[ṭ]	
yodh			Ι	[y]	arm/hand
kaph			Κ	[k]	palm of hand
lamedh			Λ	[l]	goad/crook
mem			Μ	[m]	water
nun			Ν	[n]	snake
samekh			Ξ	[s]	
ʿayin			Ο	[ʿ]	eye
pe			Π	[p]	
tsade			Ϻ[2]	[ṣ]	
qoph			Ϙ[3]	[q]	
reš			Ρ	[r]	head
šin			Σ	[š]	
taw			Τ	[t]	mark (?)

Thamudic

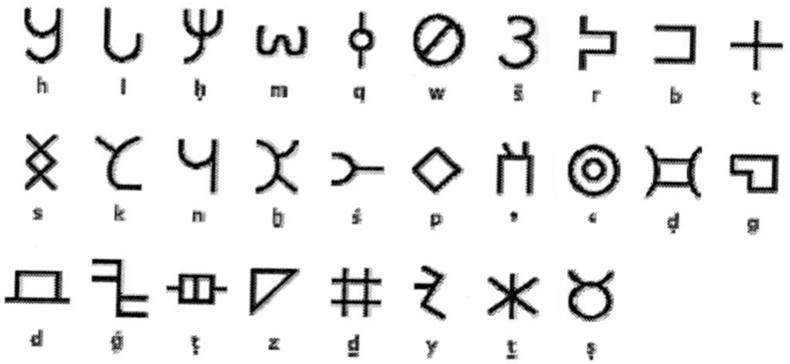

h l ḥ m q w š r b t

s k n ḫ ś p ʾ ʿ ḍ g

d ġ ṭ z ḏ y ṯ ṣ

APPENDIX

Possible Exercise Solutions:

SYMBOL	ENGLISH	EXPLANATION
	court	C for court and roof for building
	police	First letter of word
	health	Symbol often used by chemists – snake wrapped around a stick
	person	Stick man
	accident	Large cross to indicate collision / accident
	danger	Simplified symbol for dangerous goods
	police station	P for police and roof for building
	hospital	Symbol for health and roof for building

	weapon	Sword
	blood	Symbol of droplet with b inside for blood
SocS	Social Services	First three letters of first word and first letter of second word
	water	Waves
	interpreter	Head with letter i instead of mouth
	hear	Ear
	walk	Legs and feet
	ambulance	Symbol for health on top of symbol for vehicle
	thought	Head with two bubbles to show thoughts

	car	Symbol for vehicle and C for car
	lorry	Symbol for vehicle and L for lorry
	protection	Umbrella for protection
	help	Symbol for protection with helping hand

Reading List

Books on Note-taking

Rozan, J. (2004) *Note-taking in Consecutive Interpreting*, Cracow: Tertium Society for Language Studies

2 German-language Publications:

Matyssek, H. (2006) *Handbuch der Notizentechnik für Dolmetscher Teil 1*, Tübingen: Julius Groos Verlag

Matyssek, H. (2006) *Handbuch der Notizentechnik für Dolmetscher Teil 2*, Tübingen: Julius Groos Verlag

Books on Interpreting

Phelan, M. (2001) *The Interpreter's Resource*, Clevedon: Multilingual Matters Ltd.

British Association of Community Interpreters. (1989) *Guide to Good Practice*. Cambridge.

Wadensjö, C; (1995) *"Recycled Information as a Questioning Strategy: Pitfalls in Interpreter- Mediated Talk"* in Proceedings of "The Critical Link, Interpreters in the Community", Carr et al (eds) Amsterdam, John Benjamins. Pp 35-52.

Cambridge, Jan /The Linguist, NRPSI Newsletter (2001) *"Interpreting for the Public Services"*. Free publication from www.rln-northwest.com/shop free publications

Mikkelson, H. (1996) *Community Interpreting an emerging profession*, Interpreting, Vol. 1, no. 1:125-129

Corsellis, A; (1995). *"Training Needs of Public Personnel Working with Interpreters"*. In Proceedings of "The Critical Link, Interpreters in the Community", Carr et al (eds) Amsterdam, John Benjamins. Pp77-89.

Cambridge, Jan (2004) *Public Service Interpreting: Practice and Scope for Research.*

Carr, S.E. (1995) The *Critical Link: Interpreters in the Community*

Books on Dialogue Interpreting/Liaison Interpreting

ed. Mason, I. (2001) *Triadic Exchanges – Studies in Dialogue Interpreting*, Manchester: St. Jerome Publishing

ed. Mason, I. (1999) *Dialogue Interpreting*. Special Issue of The Translator, Manchester: St. Jerome Publishing

Wadensjö, C. (1998) *Interpreting as interaction*. On dialogue interpreting in immigration hearings and medical encounters. Longman Pub Group. ISBN 0582289106

Books on Terminology Work

Sager, J.C. (1990) *A Practical Course in Terminology Processing,* Amsterdam: John Benjamins Publishing Company